MY CORNER OF THE RING

MY CORNER OF THE RING

JESSELYN SILVA

AS TOLD TO BRIN STEVENS   A MEMOIR FROM A CHAMP

putnam

G. P. PUTNAM'S SONS

G. P. PUTNAM'S SONS
an imprint of Penguin Random House LLC, New York

G. P. Putnam's Sons is a registered trademark of Penguin Random House LLC.

Visit us online at penguinrandomhouse.com

Library of Congress Cataloging-in-Publication Data is available upon request.

Printed in the United States of America.
ISBN 9780525518402

1   3   5   7   9   10   8   6   4   2

Design by Eileen Savage.
Text set in Glosa Text.

This book is dedicated to my loving family,
coach, friends, and everyone who has
supported me along the way. Thank you!

MY CORNER
OF THE RING

ONE

THE PLAYGROUND

This is the only blood I want to see from you today." Then came the yank.

I stared at the baby tooth Papi had just pulled from my mouth, small and delicate like a little pearl in his large hand, and I thought that pinch of pain was probably nothing compared with what was about to happen.

"Your mouthpiece should fit better now without that wiggly tooth," Papi said, tucking it into his jeans pocket for safekeeping. My father was good at keeping calm in moments when he knew I was nervous.

It was a cool fall day in Edgewater, New Jersey, but inside Jim's Gym (commonly referred to as The Jim) it was a steam bath. Guys had stopped their training routines to watch "the girl" box. "The girl" . . . as if I were some carnival curiosity.

"The girl is gonna get trounced," I heard a teenaged boy say to his friend as I walked to the boxing ring.

I wanted to make some in-your-face comeback, but I stayed silent. I mean, he was probably right. I'd been training for only two months, and what business did I have fighting a ten-year-old boy when I had so little experience? Plus, I was only seven years old, and because I was tiny for my age, I looked even younger. People told me I was too young, too little to box. But what did they know?

What they didn't know was that I'd never shied away from a challenge. In fact, the harder the challenge, the better. Papi said that when I was a baby, whenever anyone tried to help me, I'd say, "No, me, I do it!" It became a joke in the family. I don't know where bravery comes from. Maybe you're just born with it. For me, bravery happened because I didn't like the feeling of being afraid; I much preferred the feeling of being strong, so when I thought something might be scary, I would go after it and tackle it head-on before it got

> **For me, bravery happened because I didn't like the feeling of being afraid; I much preferred the feeling of being strong.**

the better of me. I guess if there were actually ever a monster under my bed, that monster would be in trouble.

I remember when I first got into boxing, coming to it
with a rush of adrenaline, nervousness, and excitement.
Watching two people box was like nothing I'd ever seen
before: two people facing their fears and being brave.
Maybe that's why they call the boxing ring "the playground." Grown men came here to get their noses busted
and their egos shattered, but they also came to play with
their fears. I knew why most people thought this was no
place for a little kid, but to me it was the best playground
I'd ever been to in my entire life.

But when you're in the ring, facing your opponent,
even the toughest person gets the butterflies.

Another teenaged boy cracked a joke that I couldn't
hear—just the peal of laughter that followed.

Focus. Focus.

"They're just messin' with your head, Jess." That was
my trainer, Paulie. He was fitting me with the smallest
boxing equipment he could find. Paulie was my very first
boxing coach. He was this tough middle-aged African
American guy with all-white hair and baggy pants. I liked
him a lot—even though he cursed a lot.

"Here. It's my niece's headgear." He placed it loosely over
my head. "Can you see okay?" He already knew the answer.

His niece was fifteen.

Even when I tucked all of my long brown hair under the helmet, it was still loose.

"No," I mumbled. I was barely able to see past the rim.

"Good!" He gave a firm tap on my head.

I had watched Ali face off against Frazier in an old fight on TV, and they weren't wearing headgear. From my angle now, that seemed crazy.

Paulie hollered to the group of boys, "Jess is ready for a throwdown!" I thought I was ready to take someone down, but judging by my dad's body language, I could tell he wasn't so sure. There was a 50 percent chance of a throwdown, 50 percent chance I got between the ropes and forgot everything I had learned.

I'd never sparred with a boy before, and I'm pretty sure my opponent had never sparred with a girl. Actually, I'd never sparred with anyone before. When you first start training, you shadowbox. At seven years old, that's all I'd ever done—box my own shadow. A few jabs with the coach, some basic practice rounds with a couple other kids, but nothing close to a one-on-one match.

The boy I was about to spar with had a funny little cupcake of an Afro and was older by three years, and stronger; he was also much taller than I expected, which meant my uppercuts might not hit exactly where I wanted them to. I'd have to adjust. I'd learn on the fly.

"Here she is," I heard his coach say to the boy on the other side of the ring, gesturing in my direction. The boy was pacing back and forth in his corner like a garbage-tipping raccoon, his back to me. Anxious, unsure. He nodded to his coach a few times before looking over. But the moment he saw me, he chuckled in relief. Then something crossed his mind and his face froze. What if he lost to me? A little girl! I guess it would have been harder for him to lose to me than for me to lose to him. Secretly, everybody fears the underdog. I was definitely the underdog.

Still, he was sweating it. I could see it glistening on his forehead. Or maybe it was just the Vaseline on his face. I figured he was probably wondering how to hit a girl—low and tough, but not too tough. Actually I really had no idea what he was thinking. It looked like we were both a little anxious, but for different reasons. If I won, it would be a shocker, and if he lost, it would be a shocker.

"Don't be nervous, Gregie! You got this!" his mother, dressed up for the occasion, cheered below the ropes.

Papi adjusted my gloves and slipped in my mouthpiece as I listened to last-minute advice from Paulie: *Make sure you bring the punches back to your face, where you can block better, make sure to keep your head constantly moving, don't be a still target, you wanna be moving and avoid punches.* But it went in one ear and out the other. The wobbly headgear made me feel like a bobblehead figurine. And that's the last thing I wanted to feel like: one solid strike and my head would pop off.

Paulie called us to the center of the ring for a quick review of basic rules. The boy, Greg, made it to the center of the ring much faster than I did and looked a little smug as he waited for me to meet him. As I got closer to him, I could see that he was much chubbier than I'd expected. Maybe his swings would be slow, I reasoned. Maybe he would be sluggish and flat-footed. Papi had told me to think about my strengths when I boxed. Even if I couldn't reach his face, maybe my little, fast body was my strength.

Paulie would be the "ref" for the sparring match. If it were an actual sanctioned match, we'd have an official referee, but he did both jobs as coach and referee with fairness. Paulie finished going over the rules, Greg and I bumped fists—as is the traditional way to start a match—and then we moved back to our corners.

"Three rounds, one and a half minutes each round. You good with that?"

Paulie looked at me. He could tell I was a ball of nerves. His face seemed to say, *You don't have to do this, you know.*

It's hard to talk when you're wearing a mouthpiece, but loudly so my opponent could hear I managed to get out, "Yeah, three rounds, we're good with that."

Paulie nodded. He knew I was ready.

"Hey, I hear the boy puked right before he came out here," Papi said, giving me a big smile. He always had a way of making me laugh. But the truth was, Papi looked nervous, too.

A few teenaged boys were at the side of the ring making woof-woof sounds to amp up the intensity of the match. I shook my limbs and bounced up and down to warm up. My heart was beating out of my chest. I imagined my little tooth in Papi's pocket telling me, *Time to grow up! Time to grow up!*

I looked over at my father on the other side of the ropes. Maybe there were just ropes between us, but it felt like he was miles away. His mouth was moving silently. He was probably praying, hoping I wouldn't get hurt. He didn't want me in this ring. I wanted to be here. He didn't think I was ready to fight. I did. This was all me, all my doing.

"You got this," he called, pumping his fist in the air.

I got this, I said to myself. *I got this*. But there had been a quiver and hesitation in his voice that made my stomach sink.

> **" I GOT THIS. "**

Ready, I said to myself, hitting my gloves together, almost panting with anticipation and fear.

The timer was set for one and a half minutes for the round. I would have thirty seconds of rest between rounds. The green light meant the start of the fight, yellow meant final thirty seconds of the round, red meant the round was over.

My eyes were trained on the red light. Red light. Red light.

The bell rang, the red light switched to green, and the woof-woof boys on the side faded into darkness. The timer faded into darkness. Paulie faded into darkness. All I saw was Greg pushing off the ropes and lunging toward me. Then it became real.

He came out slow, as I expected, but jabbed at me fast and hard. Three quick punches. I wasn't expecting his hands to be so quick. I covered my face as best I could. Then he threw me some hard overhands. Whoa. Definitely wasn't expecting that.

"Work your right," his coach said. "Hit her hard."

In that moment I wasn't just a girl, but a competitor. I liked the feeling of that. Briefly. Then Greg got one hard punch in and I heard my father yell, "Cover your face, Jess! Keep your hands close to your chin!"

Fighters say you never forget your first hard hit in the ring against your first opponent. I'm not talking first jabs or light punches—I'm talking the first glove-to-the-face *bam!* punch of your career that forces you to ask yourself if you really want to do this for the rest of your life. The force caught me off guard, but it didn't hurt. I had taken my first real punch, and all it did was get me angry. So I started to hit back. Hard and wildly.

I realized pretty quickly that Greg was too tall for me to get a good punch to land even near his face, and I was frustrated.

"Good footwork, good footwork," his coach said as I tried to dodge.

My strategy that day would need to be more protect than punch, I decided, until I could figure out how to get in closer.

Greg hit me again.

My father hollered, then cursed in Spanish.

Underneath all this padding, I was just his little girl. It was probably weird for him to watch his only daughter, his angel, his sweetheart, enter a situation where her entire face could get smashed in.

Greg smelled gross. Every now and then he'd step away from me and cough this dry, ugly cough through his gummy mouthpiece, but it still felt too close to me, and his large body was slick with boy sweat, which, for the record, was very different from girl sweat. Boy sweat was like a nasty pee smell. Girl sweat smelled like shampoo—at least that's how I saw it . . . but of course girls always think boys smell bad, and boys always think girls have cooties. Then between coughs he'd wipe his runny nose into his gloves. I wondered if his intimidation tactic was to be a smelly boy.

Every boxer uses intimidation tactics. I'd seen intimidation tactics on TV when I watched old boxing matches with Papi and my great-grandfather late at night. Everyone had their "thing." George Foreman would sneer at his opponents. Mike Tyson would give a killer stare down. Aaron Pryor would point his glove right at his opponent before the bell rang and just stare and stare and stare. Sugar Ray Robinson used his baby face and elegance to mislead his opponents.

I didn't have any intimidation tactics. Probably would have been good to think up some fast.

I tried to concentrate on my breathing and my feet, but, *crack*, again he hit me, really, really hard this time, and I fell off balance. Maybe the first hard punch had gotten me angry, but now I was starting to feel the pain of his follow-up hits and my body began to react to them—my arms felt weak, and my legs started to shake as I attempted to swing a few more punches. Mentally I stood tough, but physically I was looking for a break.

The green light turned to yellow and I started to cry

a little—muffled whimpers through headgear. The thirty seconds until the yellow light turned to red seemed like a lifetime.

Don't do that, I kept telling myself. *Whatever you do, don't be a crybaby.*

Also, let me be perfectly clear here: I wasn't crying because I was hurt, I was crying because I was frustrated. But I was relieved when Greg backed away and gave me space. I kept my face covered and stood there waiting for the red light. Mostly, I just didn't want anybody to see that I was crying. When Paulie asked me if I was okay, I nodded that I was fine, but then I burst into tears so hard, my mouthpiece popped out.

The gentle bell that stopped the round was a little *ding* like the kind of bell that chimes to say, *Your meatball sub is ready for pickup*. It seemed out of place for a boxing ring, but I was relieved to hear it.

I was sobbing big tears before I even returned to my corner.

"Jesselyn!" My father tried reaching into the ring but was restrained by the ropes.

"Do you want to quit?" Paulie asked.

I didn't know how to answer him. For a second I clung to the ring post, thinking I should leave. Did I want to quit?

I kind of did, but I already knew that if I quit then, I'd

be a quitter for the rest of my life. Was I really going to stop after only a couple of minutes?

"Here, she needs water," Papi said.

The cool water was a relief to my dry mouth.

"Jess," Paulie said anxiously. "Should we throw in the towel?"

I think he was weighing the ramifications of allowing, even encouraging, a newbie seven-year-old girl to spar with a much bigger, much more experienced ten-year-old boy. I would learn through the years that coaches aren't gods and make bad decisions just as frequently as the athletes they're coaching.

I didn't like my headgear because it was too big on my head and it covered my eyes and made it hard to see punches coming. I hated Greg's lazy, slow but strong movements. He was too tall for me to reach up and get in a good uppercut to the chin. I didn't yet know how to lean into my opponent to find fighting space to jab. I didn't like how he breathed on me, he was so smelly, and I couldn't always hear what Paulie was saying when I was fighting because he was speaking too quietly. My mouthpiece was uncomfortable and the punches were jarring. So yes, I wanted to quit, but no, I didn't want to quit.

"What's it going to be, Jess? Fifteen seconds before the green light," said Paulie.

"No. I'm okay." I tried to control my tears. "But I can't get a punch in!" I started crying again anyway.

"Snap with the jab, don't punch," Paulie said coolly.

Greg had barely taken a break and was already standing and ready to go.

His proud mother was cheering, "Come on, sweetie! Go, sweetheart!"

I don't know why, but hearing Greg's mom root for him made me angry. I wanted my father to be cheering instead of worrying. I wanted to be the top dog, not the underdog. I wanted to be the kid boxer, not the girl crybaby. And yes, I would have also liked my mother there. But she was living in Florida at the time.

I figured the only way to feel better was to stop crying and go back in.

I wiped my tears and was up and ready again. "Let's go!" I said.

Coach Paulie shook his head and put in my mouthpiece.

Red light. Red light. Red light. Bell . . . Green light!

I came in fast in the second round, and he came in slowly again. Another intimidation tactic I'd learn about later in my boxing career: make them come to you. I threw the first jab, and it was a strike! Right to his jaw. Not hard enough to move him back, but it did startle him. And it felt goooood.

POW!

There are two ways to describe how you feel when you've given someone a clean uppercut to the jaw: terror and pleasure. I read in school that both feelings live in the same part of your brain. So there I was, caught between pleasure and terror when he hit me with a powerful right-hand *pow* to the face. He hit me so hard, my head snapped back. A boxer with more experience would have foreseen this or recovered. But I burst into tears and covered my face again. My father was silent. Greg's mother shrieked and grabbed her cheeks. "Are you ready to quit?!" Paulie yelled. Judging by the terrified look on all their faces, the correct answer would have been yes.

"No!" I heaved through tears. "No!"

"Come on, Jess!" Papi pleaded.

Paulie couldn't stop me. Papi couldn't stop me. Greg didn't want to stop me. Nobody could stop me. We were still fighting when the yellow light came on. Then red. Bell. Round two was over. I had survived two rounds. One more round to go.

In my corner, during the quick thirty-second break, I stared in shock. Papi held my water bottle, my coach held my mouthpiece. They were yelling things to each other, then yelling at each other. And

telling me things that didn't make sense. I thought I was going to hyperventilate.

"Let's end this at two rounds," Paulie said.

If I quit after two rounds, it would all be over—and by *it*, I'm not just talking about my fight with the boy. If I quit now, the whole thing would be over: my chance to get into the ring again, to ever fight in a real sanctioned match, to go even further with this sport that I had quickly grown interested in. I thought about the first time I put on boxing gloves. I remember it gave me an immediate sense of strength that I had never felt before. My love of boxing grew from there as I developed my craft. If I stopped now, I would be ending my chances of being a boxer forever. And no one but me would second-guess it if I never came back to the ring again. Maybe I was crazy to enter the big playground at first, but I was there, and I wasn't coming there to play.

I saw my idols, giants and legends in my mind, dance with arrogance in the ring. They made it look so easy. But when you're actually up there staring at a hard fist coming at you, it's a different story. I still wasn't ready to quit, though. I didn't care if I was just a little girl crying in a corner. If that's how it was going to go down, I figured the worst that could happen would be that I would go down crying. They wouldn't let me die out there, so I couldn't quit. I wouldn't quit. If I quit, I would have learned nothing.

And I had more to learn. More to figure out. More punches to give, and fewer punches to take. More crying to do. I knew this was my sport—the one that somehow seemed to be choosing me as much as I was choosing it, and the sport that I wanted to dedicate my life to. People might have thought I was too young at the time to know—"No seven-year-old knows what they want to do with the rest of their life"—but I knew. I had known the second I'd put on the gloves a few months earlier when my father let me try on his. I'd slipped them on and hollered jokingly "I'm queen of the world!" But now I wasn't joking. The gloves, the ring, the fight, even the fear made me feel bigger than I had ever felt in my entire life. And it was this fear and frustration and rush of adrenaline that had drawn me further in to this crazy world of boxing.

"Jess," Paulie said to me. "Come on, let's end this at two . . . call it quits."

I stared at the center of the ring. I looked around the gym at all the boys and men shadowboxing and punching speed bags. I saw Greg's mom wearing a pretty outfit with a shiny necklace and high heels, cheering him on from the side. I imagined myself one day standing on the side in a pretty outfit and high heels cheering someone else on, and I thought, *No, the center of that ring needs me.* I thought of the images we had seen in school of the Romans and Greeks fighting each other. The images were all of men. I thought of the boxing movies and classic boxing matches I'd watched with my father and great-grandfather. All men.

Where were all the girls? Even at seven years old it was pretty clear to me that this was a sport dominated by boys. But at that moment, in the ring, all I wanted to do was prove that a little seven-year-old has a shot at beating a bigger ten-year-old.

Red light. Red light. Red light.

"No, put in my mouthpiece." I stood up. "I'm not done." My body wobbled a little as I rose, but I shook it off.

"Oh geez . . . That girl's got no quit in her!" Papi said. And for the first time that day, he cracked a smile, even chuckled. It was worth the pain to see him proud of me.

"Hey," one of the boys ringside said, "Jess is going back in!"

"*Chica loca!*" another boy responded.

More woof-woof boys started to gather around the ring chanting and cheering. Men and boys stopped their training routines to take notice. I couldn't tell if they were rooting for me or Greg, but it didn't matter.

My biceps were tight and my right thumb was throbbing and I felt crampy in both calves. Red light, red light, red light. Green . . .

Greg came out with speed this time.

"That's it, honey!" his mother called from the side. I wasn't prepared for this. Instinct drove me back to my corner.

The crowd of boys laughed and threw their hands in the air; they expected this from a girl. I looked at my father. He no longer looked worried. He looked angry—not at me, but at a scene that seemed to be so clearly divided between boy versus girl. He said nothing. But our eyes met, and I went back in to meet the boy in the center of the ring. I didn't think about what was going to happen next. I just knew that I didn't want to quit. I didn't need to win. I wasn't going to win. All I needed to do was stay in the ring one and a half more minutes and finish. I could handle that.

The third round didn't go well. Greg stopped hitting so hard. But he still threw a lot of jabs. I was worn out from crying, and kept missing punches. The boy got the better of me pretty quickly that last round, and I ended up leaving the ring in tears. (Again!) But I did stay in until the gentle bell rang.

After the fight, Paulie patted me on the head and said, "You got guts, Jess. That'll take you far in this sport."

Somehow it didn't feel reassuring.

★ ★ ★

THE FEELING OF mutually agreeing to punch a stranger is weirdly exciting. You know you're about to start something where at least one of you could get hurt. But it's not just about the hits. It's more about pushing past fear. After the fight I lay on the floor of the gym bathroom in complete misery. My ego was hurt more than my body. My skills were clumsy; I wasn't as experienced at boxing as I wanted to be. My coach, Paulie, had told me what a dynamo I was during training sessions, but out in the ring I had felt naïve and unprepared. And I was embarrassed. I didn't want to face the people in the gym.

It wasn't just that Greg was bigger and stronger. It was that I had such a long way to go. I was too slow in my technique and too wild in my mind. I was learning that even if you think you can do something and people have told you you're pretty good at it, maybe it's not true. That's how I was feeling. Not very good. I'd thought that even if I didn't get a good punch in, at least I'd end the fight feeling tough. But I felt the opposite of tough—it's hard to feel tough when you leave the ring feeling weak.

I stood up, washed my face, and looked in the mirror. My cheeks were swollen and red, but not from fighting—from crying.

How on earth had I gotten here anyway?

★ ★ ★

TWO MONTHS EARLIER, before I ever knew what boxing was, Papi had loaded up my little brother, Jesiah, and me in the car one day after school and told us we were heading to Edgewater, a few towns over, to do something a little different. My brother was so excited, he ran back into his room and grabbed his binoculars. Edgewater is known for its dramatic undercliffs along the Hudson River and hazy views of the Manhattan skyline. But the coolest thing about Edgewater is its monk parakeets.

Rumor has it that back in the 1960s, a crate from South America full of beautiful small green parrots was damaged while being unloaded from a plane at John F. Kennedy airport. The whole flock of parakeets escaped its intended fate in dreary pet shops throughout New York City, and instead ended up in the trees of Edgewater. No one could figure out how they survived the harsh conditions, but there they remained. All along Memorial Park you could see huge four-foot-tall stick nests where the birds lived. Jesiah, with his binoculars around his neck, and I assumed when Papi said we were heading to Edgewater that he meant to see the parakeets.

Instead, he took us to a boxing gym. The Jim was dark. Dank. Small. Uninviting. Smelled like feet. Full of sweaty men. Jesiah was disappointed and grumpy when we showed up. I wasn't very interested either, at first. Papi took us to the kids' corner, gave Jesiah his iPhone, and told him to play a video game while he warmed up in the ring. I pulled out my sketchpad to draw. I loved to draw. It relaxed me and I was always surprised to see what ideas I could bring to life. My father gave me the sketchpad to doodle on when I was bored, but I had started to take the pad with me when we were driving around doing errands or driving to and from school. I looked up at my father, who was now moving around the ring doing simple jabs, and I started to sketch him.

My father had been pretty stressed out, always tired, always worried about work and bills and grown-up stuff and getting us to and from school.

Papi

By: Jesselyn

A friend had suggested he try boxing to relieve his stress and get some exercise. Jim's was the only place within a half hour's drive that allowed kids in the facility while adults trained. So dark, smelly Jim's it was. The ring wasn't even in the cen- ter of the gym. You'd think in a boxing gym the ring would be at the center, but it kind of seemed like an afterthought in this place.

The first time I saw my father box, it wasn't beautiful, but it was magical. He was smiling, dancing, light on his feet. And strong. Free and determined. I mean, don't get me wrong, he was a terrible boxer, but there's something about a person taking a punch and giving a punch: I swear you see their soul. I swear it. They allow themselves to get beaten down, to experience a sense of defeat in their bodies, but through that, find their strength at the same time. I'd never seen a sport like that before. As I became more familiar with boxing, I started to see something else. All boxing gyms have it—a lavender sort of dust that floats around, like passion, like something big is being released into the air. Like something big is happening inside a person when they fight. It's about building order and discipline. Your body is telling you to stop, but you can't, and that builds character. And I wanted it. All of it. This was the kind of playground that made sense to me. I studied every move and countermove, processing every instruction. I was the only kid in the kids' corner not glued to an iPhone. I was glued to the boxing ring. I decided to ask my dad if I could have a turn out there.

"Hey Papi, can I put on a pair of gloves?"

"Is it cool if she puts on a pair of gloves and hits the bag?" Papi asked Paulie.

"Sure—" Paulie started to say.

But without waiting for an answer, I was up and standing next to my father. I slipped on his loose-fitting gloves and practiced the moves I'd just seen.

"Hey, are you a leftie, Jess?" Paulie asked.

"My whole life," I responded.

"You're lucky. You got the southpaw advantage."

"What's that?" I asked.

"Here. Let me show you." Paulie bent down a little into a stance.

"See, most fighters are righties, so they lead with their right hand. Your strength is in your left side. So look, you have a left stance like this. Your right foot is your front foot, and your left foot is back, like this." He showed me, then continued, "Your right hand is your jab hand, your left hand is your power hand. That's a pretty good advantage if you're a boxer because most opponents won't be used to a power hit coming from the left. Get it?" I nodded, then paused. "What if you're a rightie?" I asked.

"If you're a rightie, you usually have an orthodox stance. Like this." Then he showed me what that looked like.

"But here, let me see you stand in a southpaw stance."

I caught on right away.

"Good!" Paulie said. "Now let me see you throw a punch." And with that, I landed a solid straight left punch in his gut.

I guess I was pretty good, because both my father and Paulie looked at each other in surprise.

That was the day I became a boxer.

TWO

A DIFFERENT KIND OF FIGHT

People asked me where I got my fighting spirit, and I would tell them it runs in the family.

Some people say every boxer has a story about struggle that brought them to the ring in the first place. I think the struggle came generations before me.

My grandparents on both sides were immigrants. My father was named after his father, Pedro, who was named after his father, Pedro, and his father, Pedro. My brother's a Pedro, but he goes by his middle name, Jesiah. There are a lot of Pedros in my family. I'm one of the few girls in the family, and the only Jesselyn. My grandmother joked that our ancestors were good at making boys but bad at raising them.

Papi's father, my grandfather, came over on a packed

lobster boat from the port of Mariel, Cuba, in 1980 when he was twenty years old. He couldn't stand the smell of shellfish after that. I never actually met him before he died, but I've always felt like I understood his fight to get to America and his struggle in America.

Like many Cubans coming to the United States at that time, my grandfather sought freedom from the powerful rulers of his country. Visions of the American dream drew him to this land. But his overseas trip here wasn't easy. The ocean was rough, the skies were dark, and the small fishing boat was so weighed down with people that every wave crashed hard on top of its passengers, leaving them wet, dehydrated, and afraid. Fearing the vast sea surrounding them, my grandfather once told my father, was a blessing in disguise, because it made them forget about their hungry bellies and various sicknesses, and the horrible filth and stench inside the vessel. He said he was one of the lucky ones. That on more than one occasion they passed travelers in rafts as small as five feet long with nothing more than a bottle of rum and a bucket of water.

Once their fishing boat hit the Florida Straits, sharks started to appear, looking for people to grab off flimsy boats. He said it wasn't a shock when passengers saw a human leg float past. Their trip took fifteen hours, but in that time people on the boat had already started to hallucinate—probably because of a combination of dehydration and hypothermia.

When my weary grandfather landed in Florida, he approached a young Hispanic man sitting on the dock and asked him in Spanish, "Where are we?" The young man handed him a Dr Pepper and said in perfect English, "Welcome to the United States of America!" That was the first time my grandfather realized how hard it was going to be to live in a country where he didn't speak, read, or write the language. I often wondered what it would have been like to be my grandfather. When someone asked him a direct question, he would smile and nod and not be able to answer because he didn't understand. He was forced to speak in one-word sentences—"Yes" or "No"—when he couldn't follow along.

My grandfather's first job was driving a taxi for Good Cab in Union City, New Jersey.

"Always respect the customers," his boss would say to him in Spanish. "Always be polite, even if the customer doesn't tip. And always, *always* drive safely! One car accident and you're fired."

Good Cab was where my grandfather met my grandmother. She was the beautiful dispatcher at the cab company and had arrived in the United States from Ecuador a few years earlier with a similar story of leaving the familiarities of home and leaving loved ones behind to start a new life in an unfamiliar land, except instead of traveling by boat, she had landed in New York by airplane. In one hand she had a suitcase, in the other were her tattered identification papers, and in her belly was a growing baby. She was sixteen years old and found herself standing on the sidewalk of the terminal with no one to pick her up and nowhere to go. Tears streamed down her face, and she wondered if she'd made a terrible mistake by leaving her family in hopes of a new life for herself and her future son.

My grandfather and grandmother had a lot in common: they both felt lost, struggling to make it in a strange new land, both trying to better their lives.

They became a couple soon after they met. And then things happened quickly. My father, my grandmother's second son, was born within a year, and eleven months later my father's brother Samuel was born. With three young boys and not much money, the American dream felt more like a nightmare. The stress of having little money and living in a cramped apartment caused a lot of worry.

When I asked my father what his father was like, he simply said, "I don't remember much about him. He wasn't around a lot."

Later I found out that my grandfather left his job as a taxi driver and turned to a life of crime—or as my grandmother called it "the underworld jobs." His underworld job was to steal things and sell them on the street. He ended up in jail many times. To my father, his father was always in and out of his life—one month showering him with attention, another month just gone.

When Papi was seven years old, he developed asthma. On more than one occasion, something affected his lungs, and his mother had to take him to an asthma specialist quite a few times. Then came the medication: inhalers and nasal sprays, both of which he hated to take. Nothing seemed to help him, but eventually he learned to cope with it.

One birthday, his father appeared out of nowhere with a white rusty used BMX bike for him—still, it was the most beautiful bike my father had ever seen, because it was his! Papi had never received such a nice birthday gift from his father, so it came as quite a happy surprise. Maybe his father's new underground job was paying off and things for his family were headed in the right direction.

But then his father told him he needed to share his bike with his little brother, which disappointed Papi. And because the bike didn't come with training wheels, Papi had to learn how to ride it on his own without any aid.

My father never celebrated another birthday after that year.

★ ★ ★

WE DIDN'T MAKE a big deal about birthdays in our house—at least not like most families. Maybe it had something to do with my father's childhood, but he was firm in never going overboard with those kinds of things.

"There's no need to go crazy with birthdays," he'd say. "We can celebrate each other *every* day, not just that one day."

At school a girl once said to me, "My mom says your dad doesn't throw birthday parties for you because men don't know how to plan parties."

I knew that was what some people thought. There are stereotypes about single dads raising their kids, and really big stereotypes about guys like my dad—Latino, night-shift guys, with tattoos. But some people were really wrong when it came to assuming things about other people. It always surprised visitors when they came over to my house and it was immaculate. The laundry was always folded perfectly. Meals were hot and fresh and yummy. Beds were made. For my father, our house was our kingdom, and he kept it pristine.

No, we didn't do birthday parties with streamers and balloons like a lot of kids. Instead my father would take

Jesiah and me and my uncle out to play video games and eat ice cream at Dave and Buster's. I'd play Subway Surfers until kids yelled at me to get off. When the night was over, he'd hand me an envelope with birthday cash inside.

"Here, don't spend it all in one place."

"I won't spend it *any*place," I'd respond each time.

"That's the right answer."

I wanted to buy new boxing gloves. Then I thought about my sketch pad, every page filled with drawings of people and cartoon characters—mostly superheroes—and thought maybe I'd buy a new sketch pad, maybe some watercolor paints as well, since I'd started getting interested in painting and it would have been fun to have my own paint set. But instead I saved every penny. The only one in my family to ever go to college and graduate was my grandmother. I wanted to go to college, too. So I saved.

Birthday nights out, really any night out with Papi, were extra special for Jesiah and me. Most nights my father was getting ready to head out for work. When I began elementary school, he switched from a day job to working the night shift, which started at 11:00 p.m. and ended at 6:30 a.m. By 8:00 a.m. he was back home, showered, making breakfast, packing lunches, and taking us to school. By 9:00 a.m. he was in bed. He'd sleep until 2:00 p.m. so that he could be rested and ready to pick us up and take us to after-school activities, more and more often to the boxing gym. Then it would start all over again.

Poor Papi was tired a lot. My father's chest pain began when he started working the night shift. Stress and lack of sleep can affect the body in dangerous ways, especially when you're so busy caring for others that you forget to care for yourself.

Sometimes people asked me if being raised by a single dad was like being raised by a single mom. Sure, some people may have thought when I was younger that it was weird to have my father come check on me in the women's bathroom at a restaurant, instead of a mom, but it just seemed like raising kids alone was hard work in general.

With eyes covered, he would yell from just inside the door, "Jesselyn, did you mummify the toilet seat?"

He had taught me early on to cover the toilet seat with enough toilet paper to protect myself from germs when I sat down. But we would laugh at the amount of protective covering he thought the seat needed. We called it "mummifying."

"Papi! Yes!" I would holler back.

"Okay, don't forget to mummify!"

He really was crazy about those kinds of things.

★ ★ ★

PAPI WORKED IN the sanitation department at a beef processing plant in New Jersey. He was responsible for cleaning the machines in the factory. If you were eating a burger in New York's Lower East Side, chances are my father had bleached the grinders where that beef was processed. It wasn't a pretty job—in fact my dad said it was the grossest job he'd ever had—but it was an important one that he took seriously. Without proper sterilization, an entire day's production line of meat could be contaminated and make a lot of people very sick. Jesiah and I made up a song about salmonella that we'd sing—"Salmonella, salmonella, not ice cream vanilla"—but I don't think Papi appreciated it very much. So he went to work on time and worked hard and got promoted from bucket washer to cleaning the largest machine in the processing plant—which, he was proud to say, when done the right way, took seven hours to clean stem to stern.

One night the bosses offered free burgers to the crew. Everyone headed toward the lounge area to eat. My father stayed behind.

"Hey, you coming?" asked one of his coworkers.

"Naw, you go ahead," Papi said, scrubbing the inside of a bucket.

"What, you're holding out for steak?"

"No . . . It's just that the thought of eating this stuff makes me sick." That caused everyone in the work area to laugh. A man who dedicated his evenings to a job that made him physically ill was tough to understand. But it allowed him to be with us during the day.

Sometimes when people asked me where I got my fighting spirit, I had another answer besides it running in my family. I would give them an answer that surprised them: "I fight because sometimes I get angry."

I know I wasn't supposed to talk like that. Maybe I could think it, but people don't want to hear that you throw punches because you're upset about stuff. It was true, though. Plenty of things in my life felt unfair and got me angry. And those were the things that powered me in the ring. I hit the bag a little harder on those days. Bad days outside the gym were my best days in the gym.

I found myself getting upset about the way some people treated my father as a single dad. It seemed like an endless battle. I would see it in little ways every day.

One morning my father came home from work and needed to go see a doctor. At the time he didn't tell me he was having terrible chest pains and thought he was having a heart attack, because of course I would worry. He always said I had this crazy, irrational fear of him dying . . . which I did.

So he went to the hospital quietly and alone while my anxious grandmother played children's songs on the CD player and then drove Jesiah and me to school that morning. As had sometimes happened in the past, Jesiah forgot his lunchbox in the car, so he went down to the school office and asked one of the administrators for a lunch voucher.

"No, Jesiah, I'm not giving you a lunch voucher this time," she said. "Your father should have remembered to pack your lunch."

"My father didn't drive me today. Can you call my grandma?"

"No, Jesiah, I'm not calling your grandmother."

"But my dad is seeing a doctor," Jesiah said, starting to whimper.

After much pleading, the administrator finally called my grandmother. My
grandmother owned a cleaning business
and wasn't able to leave her work, so she
couldn't bring Jesiah's lunch to school.
Then the administrator called my father in
the hospital. They had a brief conversation.

"Well Jesiah, it looks like you'll be able to have lunch
today," the woman said. "Because I just checked with the
cafeteria, and they have an extra lunch available for you."

The truth was, I think she was being a little tough on
my brother to teach him a lesson, because he was always
forgetting his lunch at home. But for some reason, because
my father was in the hospital, this time it felt personal.

My father came home after the hospital (no heart
attack, just stress), took one look at my angry face, and
said, "Yes, I heard . . . he forgot his lunch again."

"If you were a single *mom*, no one would have been
mad if you'd forgotten to pack our lunches!"

"You don't know that. Jesiah is always leaving his lunch
at home and sometimes tough love is the only way to learn."

Later he called the principal and made the administrators aware of the struggles of being a single father, and of
how he worked just as hard as any mom would, managing
the kids, the household, and a full-time job. And how he

thought he was being discriminated against just because he was a man. Things at school changed after that—Jesiah was always given a lunch voucher without too much fuss on days he forgot his lunch.

What also drove my fighting spirit were the things that made me, like my DNA and being a girl, and the things around me, like my father's annoying night-shift job, negativity about girl boxers, school stuff, you name it.

Sometimes what drove my fighting spirit were the things that weren't around me, like my mother.

I wasn't the only one in school being raised by one parent. A bunch of my friends came from single-parent households. But I was pretty sure I was the only kid being raised by a father instead of a mother. My mother and father separated two and a half years after my brother was born. Then my mom moved down to Florida for a while looking for better work opportunities. Even though we always stayed in contact, I really missed her. When she came back a few years later, it was incredible when she would visit on weekends. She'd take us to the movies, the trampoline park, pumpkin picking . . . all the things that moms do with their kids. By the time I had started boxing, she had just moved back to New Jersey.

"What's new with you?" she asked during a trip to the zoo.

"Well," I said thoughtfully, "I've started boxing."

"Boxing? Why boxing?" she said in her no-nonsense way.

People said I was my mom's mini-me. I took that as a compliment because she was the most beautiful woman I knew. Her mixed Cuban and Puerto Rican heritage gave her the prettiest traits, like thick dark hair and almond-shaped eyes. And man, was she strong! She never played a sport in her entire life, but she was all muscle. I loved hanging out with her.

When my mother asked, "Why boxing?" that day at the zoo, it was a good question I hadn't really considered; after all, I was only seven years old. I mean, why not boxing. Truth is, it's not like I got into boxing because I was a girl and wanted to blaze a trail . . . That hadn't even occurred to me when I first picked up the gloves. I was just a kid and it looked fun! The part about proving myself as a girl boxer came a couple of years later, once I realized how few girl boxers there were in this male-dominated sport. And it wasn't until I was even older that I came to see that I not only needed to make a place for myself in this sport, but a place for all girls of all ages. Somehow.

It wasn't that I was drawn to boxing because I liked to get hit. I hated getting hit. But I loved throwing it back. And sometimes in life, especially as a little kid, and a lot

> **I could fight to prove that there was a place for me.**

of times as a girl, they don't let you throw back punches—not in school, not at home, not on an actual playground. So I boxed because even if I felt like I didn't belong there, I could fight to prove that there was a place for me.

Like my immigrant grandparents, I was learning a new language—the language of boxing. I was fighting to belong in a world that sometimes seemed strange and cold and unwelcoming. And once I got started boxing, I didn't want to be just half in, half out of the ring. I wanted to be all in.

Maybe being a fighter was in my DNA, but the hardest part of proving my DNA was still to come.

Now all I had to do was learn how to fight.

CHAPTER THREE
FIRST FIGHT WITH A GIRL

I spent two more years at The Jim after my first crybaby sparring match with Greg. In those two years I never once fought in a sanctioned match against a girl. Not because I couldn't, not because I didn't want to, but because there were no girls my age to fight. All the boy boxers were getting fights scheduled, but not me. So I focused on training hard and knew that when the day of my first sanctioned match came, I would be ready. Almost every day except Sunday—Grandma wouldn't allow me to skip church for anything. But I would have if I could have. I made a promise to myself in those two years that not only would I never shed a tear in the ring again (I had mostly kept that promise), but I would fight to win, not just defend. That meant long hours and commitment in the gym.

There were days during training that I would punch so hard, my wrists were red. Times I would beg my father to go out jogging with me so late that we ran with flashlights. In between homework and the gym I would shadowbox in my bedroom to music until Papi finally said lights-out. I must have done that hundreds of times. I sparred with boys in the gym on occasion when they were willing. In little ways I saw my body change; it was moving away from the punches faster, and my muscles were getting stronger and more defined. I was getting the basics of my technique down. Some days I felt like a ballerina learning to be graceful. Other days I felt like a bull learning to be powerful. As my skills improved, sparring with boys became a thrill, not something to fear. It made me want more. I came to like the challenge of boxing with boys who were bigger and faster. Paulie was a great trainer, and I liked him a lot. He would stop the action and explain what I was doing wrong during sparring sessions.

"Practice with your lead hand. Jab. Hook."

Over and over again. Lead hand. Lead hand. Lead hand.

Power shift. Then move forward. One direction: ahead, not back.

My moves were getting tighter.

But after two years of training, I was getting frustrated. I wanted to get in the ring and show off my skills. Finally, when I was nine years old, I confronted my father. In the car ride to the gym one afternoon I said, "I want to be a boxer."

"You are a boxer," my dad said, laughing.

"No, like an actual boxer who fights in matches."

"Okay."

"I'm sick of sparring with boys. They go to actual boxing gyms and have boxing teammates and go to tournaments and get placed in divisions. And all I do is train to box but I don't actually compete."

We pulled into the parking lot of the gym, and Papi turned to me with a serious expression and asked, "How far do you want to go with this?"

I looked him straight in the eye and said, "I want to fight in the Junior Olympics."

I had heard all the boys in the gym talk about training for the Junior Olympics. For amateur boxers in my age group, that was the ultimate national fighting competition. Only the best of the best fought in the Junior Olympics. If I worked hard, I could get there too.

My father nodded. For the first time, he understood how serious I was about this sport.

"You know what that means . . ." Papi's voice trailed off.

"Yes."

That meant we had to leave The Jim because it wasn't registered under USA Boxing and because Paulie wasn't a registered coach. The Jim was a training facility. They didn't have a team of fighters like a registered boxing gym does; it was a place where boxers came for extra gym time. I would never be able to compete as an amateur boxer at the top level if I stayed there, because we wouldn't be able to register for fights. So with heavy hearts, we left.

It was surprisingly difficult to find a good gym. We toured several. Most of the gyms we visited were dirty and crumbling or the equipment was old and unsafe. Lots of places didn't want to train kids. And lots of trainers weren't suited to training kids, especially girls. As Papi would say after meeting a particular trainer, "A little rough around the edges, that one."

The second gym we decided to try, DMG in Paterson, New Jersey, closed within two months of my training there. The third gym kicked us out because Papi didn't get along with some of the coaching staff.

One day at True Warriors, the third gym, my dad was standing at the bag giving me some tips when one of the coaches yelled to him, "Hey, you can't be on the floor where the boxers train."

"I'm just watching my daughter."

He yelled even louder. "I said you can't be on the floor!"

"Are you really talking to me that way? Because it's a little disrespectful," Papi said, getting agitated.

"Yeah, you, get off the floor and sit down!"

"I don't feel like sitting down."

Papi and the coach started to move in closer. Like I said, fighting is in my DNA, and I knew my father wouldn't back down if someone was being disrespectful.

"YOU! Sit down!" The coach moved quickly toward my father.

"No one tells me to sit down. Ever." Papi wasn't yelling, he was very calm and respectful.

Papi looked at me and back at the angry trainer and said, "We're done here." And with that, we left that gym for good with my gloves still on my hands.

Right about then I wondered if we'd ever find a gym that would take on a girl boxer . . . and my father.

★ ★ ★

THE BERGEN COUNTY Police Athletic League (PAL) in Hackensack, New Jersey, looked like a karate dojo from the outside. We'd driven by it many times because it's close to my home. Someone had suggested it might have a boxing

program. My father
wasn't convinced, but
we stopped in one day
after school.

The sign at the
entrance to the build-
ing said there were no
children under the age
of thirteen allowed. I
was only nine years old
and in the third grade.
It wasn't looking good.

"Papi, let's leave,"
I said, feeling a little
discouraged.

"Come on, Jess, we're already here."

Inside, it was crazy. The place was full of boxers—all
boys, some older, some close to my age. I had been training for two years, but I still felt unsure about the place,
even though it was bright and clean, and the people were
friendly. I couldn't believe it! This was a building we'd
driven by hundreds of times. Who knew so many cool
things were happening inside? Never judge a book by its
cover! I knew right away I was going to like it there.

Bergen County Police Athletic League (PAL)

Then we met Don Somerville, the boxing director, a super-tall, lean African American man with a gentle, soothing voice and easygoing demeanor. You'd never suspect that he'd been a fierce amateur boxing champion in his day.

Don came over to us and said curiously, "Can I help you?"

"My daughter wants to fight in the Junior Olympics, and we need a trainer who can get her there," my father said.

"Oh, I see," Don said, studying me carefully. "What's your name?" he asked me, bending down a little so I wouldn't have to strain so much to look him in the eye.

"Jesselyn," I said, sounding unusually shy.

"How many fights have you won, Jesselyn?" he continued.

"None," I said with no shyness at all.

"Okay. Well, how many fights have you lost?"

"None," I said in an even stronger tone.

"We can't find a girl her age to fight," Papi said, "and she's been training hard for two years now at different gyms. We need the right trainer and the right gym."

Don nodded. It was clear he understood. "I think I might be able to help."

Papi and Don liked each other right away because they were both huge football fans. I liked Don because he was a funny guy and laughed easily.

PAL was different from the other gyms because it drew in kids from the area who were having trouble in their lives. Don ran the gym's Suspension Alternative Program (SAP) so he knew how to work with younger boxers. SAP intervenes with kids who are struggling in school and at home. The boxing gym gave them an outlet. My dad thought that was pretty cool. Some of these kids, all boys, would be my future teammates, and in no time they would be like a second family.

"We have a team that might be just right for you," Don said.

Team? I had boxed with other kids, but I'd never been or felt like part of a team.

"I thought boxers boxed alone," I said.

What a lot of people don't realize about boxing is that at every level, even in professional boxing, fighters train as a team with the same trainer at the same gym. They become stablemates, sparring partners, travel companions, motivators, and friends. Coaches don't look to train just one great boxer; they look to build a strong team of fighters. Each team carries the reputation of the gym and its coaching staff with them to matches and tournaments. Gyms with a lot of winning fighters on their team attract better fighters to the gym. And sparring better fighters would help me get prepared for the Junior Olympics.

In order to qualify for Junior Olympics, I first had to be a registered boxer and have five registered bouts under my belt. I would be placed in the Pee Wee 9-10 division first, because of my age and weight, and advance in divisions as I got older. My path became clear. I would need to focus and push myself. It wouldn't happen overnight. It might take a few years, but I was determined to get there.

Right away Don got me going on a regular routine: heavy bag, legwork (it was all about legwork), shadow-boxing, jumping rope, running, push-ups, sit-ups, pull-ups, sparring.

I trained even harder than ever under Don. He would say anyone could be a boxer, no matter how young, no matter what sex. You just needed discipline, dedication, and most of all a desire to be great. I loved that . . . a desire to be great. I thought about that a lot. I felt like it was the most motivating thing he could have said to me. I didn't want to be a beginner boxer, or just a good boxer. I didn't want to box as a hobby or as an after-school activity. I wanted to be great! I wanted to be a legend like all those who had come before me.

People were beginning to notice my improvement. Inside the gym, boys started to respect "the girl." I think they looked forward to sparring with me, too. I became a solid competitor. Outside the gym, people started to notice something different about me as well, especially my best friend, Mackenzie. We had been best friends since kindergarten and were still best friends in the third grade. I guess I had been spending less time playing with my friends and more time training, but I hadn't really thought about it until she confronted me.

"Why can't you play anymore after school?" she asked me during class.

"Because I need to box."

"Every day?"

"Yeah, I need to train."

"What are you training for?"

"The Junior Olympics! And one day, I'm going to be the greatest female boxer in the history of boxing!"

She laughed at me. So one afternoon I brought her to the gym to show her what I did.

An hour into training she said, "It's okay, but it's not my thing." And that was the first and last time she came with me to the gym.

By the third grade, kids at school started to call me "the girl boxer." Even kids I barely knew called me that. It seemed a little awkward at first, but it was true. I was a girl, and all I wanted to do was box.

I grew envious. How could I let my friends and family call me the girl boxer when all I ever did was watch the boys in my gym box in sanctioned matches? I had to fight in at least five sanctioned matches to even qualify for the Junior Olympics, so I was starting to get antsy. And it wasn't like there was a directory of girl fighters we could rely on. We would have to wait and see if there was a girl at my level to fight. So I waited and I trained.

"Don," I would say to him after a workout, "when can I fight?"

"You are fighting," he would always respond.

"No, I mean fight fight."

According to the rules set up by USA Boxing, sanctioned

fights between boys and girls are not allowed. Boys have to fight boys. Girls have to fight girls. So I couldn't officially fight boys, just spar with them. But I was okay with that. Because at least there were girls out there fighting now. I was just impatient for some real action.

In my free time, I read a lot about boxing. A lot had changed in the world of women's boxing. In 1876, in one of the first "boxing matches" in American history, two women named Nell Saunders and Rose Harland fought each other for two hundred dollars and a silver butter dish. Saunders ended up with the purse and the butter dish, and Harland received ten dollars.  In the early days of boxing, it was hard for a woman to get a boxing license, making the history of female boxing hard to trace. In 1957, famed boxer Barbara Buttrick and her opponent Phyllis Kugler received the state of Texas's first boxing licenses for women. They went on to fight each other in a world title; Buttrick won unanimously, making her the first women's world boxing champion that same year. It wasn't until 1988 that any national boxing association gave women official approval to box when Sweden became the first country to lift a ban on women's amateur boxing. In 1993 the American Civil Liberties Union sued USA Boxing to allow women to compete in matches. The

London Olympics in 2012 was the first time that women ever boxed in the games, so our history of famous female boxers is pretty short . . . but I wanted to be on that list with Laila Ali, Cecilia Braekhus, Lucia Rijker, Mia St. John, Holly Holm, Ann Wolfe, Claressa Shields, and all the rest. Many of these women might be unknown to most people, but they're idols and legends to me and to other female boxers working hard to get where they've gone.

1875

1876
Saunders v Harland
First match

1957
Barbara Buttrick
First World Champ

1988
Sweden lifts ban on
Women's Boxing

1993
Women can
compete in USA

2012
Women's Boxing
joins Olympics

2015

I began to ask Don more and more when I could fight a girl. Then I began to beg. He would just continue the workout. "Learn how to lean in and get under."

I was getting frustrated. It was like practicing for a game or dance recital or musical concert that would never come.

I said to Don one day after a really tough training session, "Am I ready to fight now?"

Don said, "You gotta be ready all year round."

"So am I ready?"

"No, not yet."

"But how can I learn if I never get a match in the ring?"

I kept asking him, and finally he confessed. "Jess," he said, "I'm having trouble finding someone for you to fight. There just aren't any girls out there your age." But he promised me he wouldn't give up looking for the right opponent.

The right opponent would be my height and weight and match my level of experience, and there were very few girls in that category.

I started with Don in August 2015, but it wasn't until that November that he found a girl for me to fight. Three months might not seem like a very long time, but I had been training for a couple of years already and was more than ready to prove myself in the ring. One afternoon I came to the gym and Don had a huge smile on his face.

"I got a girl for you to fight."

"Really?!" I was ecstatic.

"Yep. She's just like you: same weight, same height, same level."

"How many fights?" I asked nervously.

"None. This will be her first one. She hasn't been able to find anybody to fight either. She's just like you."

Perfect!

"She's not *just* like me," I said with a wry smile. "No one's like me."

Don chuckled gently and said, "That's right, Jess: no one's like you."

A few days earlier, Don had gotten a call from the father of this girl named Carrie—he was also her coach, and she was looking for someone to spar with. Don suggested setting up an actual sanctioned fight for us. Although Carrie's dad was a little hesitant, they came by the gym a few days later. We met, hung out, and did kid stuff together, and it was settled. We were both eager to fight each other. The match would take place in a boxing ring during a Fight Night event at a high school in Carrie's hometown.

After Carrie and her dad left, Don turned to me and said, "So, do you feel good about this?"

"Yes! I'm ready!"

"You're not *quite* ready . . ."

Yes I was—more than ready.

"Naw. Something's missing."

What could possibly be missing? I thought.

"Every boxer needs a nickname."

I hadn't even thought about it. But he was right. Say the name Ray Robinson and people ask, "Who's that?" but say Sugar Ray, and everyone knows who you're talking about. All the legends had nicknames: Muhammad "the Greatest" Ali, Oscar "the Golden Boy" de la Hoya, Evander "the Real

Deal" Holyfield, Joe "the Brown Bomber" Louis. Even the kids at my gym and kids they were boxing had nicknames. I needed to come up with a nickname quickly. So the boys in the gym started to brainstorm.

> **Every boxer needs a nickname.**

At that time, Don's wife, Maria, was always at the gym. She was very kind and supportive of me and at times acted like a mother figure. She would often say, "Oh Jess, you are too cute!" Everything was "too cute." My movements were too cute, my gloves were too cute, my nail polish was too cute, my breathing sounds when I boxed were too cute. So when Don asked me what my nickname should be, all the boys in the gym said, "How about Jess 'Too Cute' Silva?" When Maria found out about my nickname, she of course said, "Oh, that is just too cute!"

The nickname stuck.

A few days later, Papi, Jesiah, and I were watching *Rocky IV* on TV. It was rated PG, so Papi made us close our eyes and cover our ears during the adult parts. There's this one scene in the movie where Apollo Creed comes out in this amazing boxing outfit dancing to "Living in America" sung by James Brown. Sylvester Stallone, playing Rocky Balboa, looks stunned, and the crowd is going wild; it's hands down the most incredible boxing entrance ever. I've actually watched every *Rocky* movie backward and forward. My father said they were the all-time best classic boxing movies.

But as I thought about Creed's entrance, I turned to my father and said, "Papi, I can't fight Carrie."

"Why not?" My father looked concerned.

"I don't have an outfit like those guys," I said, pointing to the TV.

Within a week, Papi and I were driving out to Double-A Boxing in Brooklyn to meet with a tailor. Double-A supplied all the boxers I knew with their outfits. Even the actors in the movie *Creed*—a spinoff of the *Rocky* films—got fitted there.

"Pink!" the guy at Double-A said to me. "I see you comin' off those ropes in bright pink!" he said again in a thick New York accent.

"Pink?!" I said to him. No way! I hated pink.

I decided on something tougher: black, gold, and purple.

I got to help them design it. I even got to

pick out the fabric:
satin, of course. Within
a few weeks, my out-
fit arrived. It was crazy
how legit I felt wearing
it. On the back was my
full name in gold cursive
lettering with a gold crown
above it. The front was
purple and black with a
thick gold stripe in the
middle. But the best part:
an all-gold hood. That
was for real!

I got so wrapped up
in the moment that I didn't think to ask
how Papi was going to pay for such a fancy outfit. Normally
they cost at least six hundred dollars. He said it was nothing
to worry about, that he'd gotten a good deal on it.

Later I found out he'd sold his Xbox to cover the
expenses.

"I'm a grown man. What do I need an Xbox for anymore," Papi said with a wink and a smile. But I knew that
secretly he probably missed it.

I had my first official sanctioned fight on November

6, 2015. I was nine years old. The fight took place in the gymnasium of Bloomfield High School in New Jersey. A bunch of other kids were boxing that night, but Carrie and I were the youngest, and were two of the only—if not *the* only—girls boxing. The place was done right! In the center of this big gym was a really nice black, red, and white ring. Bleachers were set up, and refs were checking the fighters in and managing last-minute changes and equipment issues. They were even selling tickets at the door. It was crazy-cool. Twenty-five dollars a head and all proceeds went to local police officers suffering from post-traumatic stress disorder, which I thought was pretty nice.

Papi and I arrived at 5:00 p.m. for weigh-in. My fight wasn't until 7:00 p.m. I definitely had butterflies.

Weigh-in is a super-important part of the sport not only because it determines which division a boxer fights in, but because it makes sure it's an even fight, which results in fewer injuries. The fight was set for the 75-pound Pee Wee 9-10 division, but the day before the match, Don called me into the gym. He told me to put on heavy sweatpants and a heavy sweatshirt and then to get on the treadmill and start running. He made me run on the treadmill for five minutes, then jump on the scale, then run on the treadmill for another five minutes, then jump on the scale. He made me do that for half an hour. Afterward Don told me the girl

I was fighting was coming in some-where between 68 and 70 pounds and we needed to be close to equal in weight. She would need to gain a few pounds, but I had to drop two to three pounds in less than a day.

-2 lbs

It turned out that at weigh-in, Carrie came in under-weight, so her mom made her eat cupcakes and drink a ton of water. She put boots on and weighed herself again. She weighed in at just under 73 pounds, so the fight was on! Luckily for her, we'd have to wait a couple of hours before our match, so her belly wouldn't feel full by the time we fought.

After weigh-in, I noticed that the seats in the gym were filling up and the crowd was getting rowdy. The light butterflies that had been fluttering in my stomach before weigh-in felt like they were riding a roller coaster now. I was really nervous!

After boxers weigh in, each one sees a doctor for a phys-ical. Doctors check blood pressure, hands, knuckles, eyes, and ears, and listen to your heart . . . that sort of thing.

I went into the girls' locker room to relax and get ready. It smelled like fresh paint. The rows of lockers had just been painted a bright cherry red, and they were shiny and new looking. For some reason the fresh paint smell and pretty color of the lockers made me smile. I looked down at my sparkly outfit, and maybe a little bit of me felt the same way—shiny, new, and strong. I twisted my hair into a tight bun and did some stretching. I was all alone, thinking about the things I had been working on in training and everything I had to remember when I got in the ring. Every boxer fears their opponents will be faster and more powerful. Part of being a good boxer is learning how to remain calm and collected before and during a fight.

Don and Papi came in to wrap my hands and give me a pep talk.

"Are you doing okay?" Don asked.

I was doing okay.

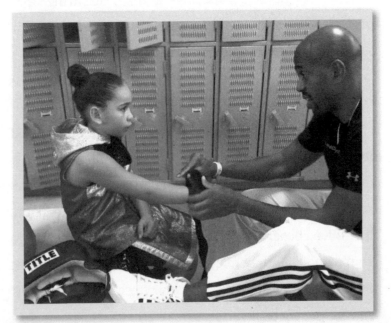

"Are *you* doing okay?" he said to my anxious father.

We all started to laugh.

Then to me, Don said, "You've been training hard for this. You're ready. I wouldn't send you out there if you weren't. So I want you to focus on one thing tonight. Just one thing: having fun!"

The gymnasium where we were fighting was on my opponent's turf. Carrie was "home," and I was the "away" player. That meant that most of the support would be for her. So I was completely shocked when I came out of the locker room and saw so many familiar faces in the stands. Paulie, my old coach, was there. A few kids from the gym were there, and several family members: both grandmothers, my uncle, my little brother, and another uncle. Knowing that I had my own small cheering section made me feel more confident. I wanted to prove myself more than ever.

Carrie and I would go three rounds. My nervousness had changed to excitement. It felt like I'd been training for a long, long time, and now I finally had a fight to show off my skills.

Hands wrapped, gloves on, headgear tight, mouthpiece in. There's an unspoken requirement in boxing that the first thing a boxer does when he or she gets into a ring is go around and stomp their foot in the direction of each judge. It's just kind of a way to say, "Thank you and I respect you" before the match begins. So I did that, and so did Carrie. Then we went back to our corners.

The announcer called my name—Jesselyn "Too Cute" Silva!—but I was so busy concentrating on what I needed to do during the match that I didn't take in all the energy of the crowd or what was going on around me. All I remember is waiting for the cue from the ref to meet in the middle. After a few minutes of talking with the judges, the referee called us to the center of the ring to greet each other and listen to his final words before the match started. My heart was racing, and my blood was flowing. I was eager to fight, but I knew better than to show it. You never wanted to show emotion in the ring—might give your opponent an idea of how you were feeling—nervous, confident, or somewhere in between.

The referee made a joke about how long it takes to start these matches, and we both laughed. Then we bumped gloves and returned to our corners.

There are no red, yellow, and green lights in sanctioned events like the ones used in sparring at a gym; there's only a bell to begin rounds and a bell to end rounds. It seemed like an eternity before the bell rang to start, but when it did, I came out hard and fast—I kind of surprised myself with my speed. I started in right away. The first punch

woke Carrie up. She covered her face with her big blue boxing gloves and kept them there for most of my punches. She was smaller and a little delicate. I stepped back and waited for her to regroup. Then I went at her again.

I felt a little uncomfortable at first, hitting someone who wasn't hitting back. Then Papi yelled from the bleachers, "Come on, Jess. Easy work." I cut under into her stomach. I could tell that one hurt her a little. *Don't retreat. Keep punching.* This was part of my training and part of growing as a boxer. I kept hitting. I nailed her with some body blows, and landed a few to her face. It felt easy because she didn't really throw too many punches back. I was on the attack, and she was playing straight defense.

The bell rang, and round one was over before it ever began.

Carrie went to her corner, and I think she might have been crying. I didn't feel terribly bad about it, because I realized that it was that first sparring match with the boy where I cried that I got my strength. This first fight was helping her become a better boxer just as much as it was making me one.

In my corner, Don said, "You're doing a good job, kiddo, good job. But don't assume that the next round will be like the first. Stay tall out there."

Boxing can be an unpredictable sport. Even weaker

fighters can take down stronger ones in just a few swipes. Sometimes when you think you know who's going to win, the fighter comes out stronger and more determined in the next round and changes the results to their advantage. That's what makes the sport exciting.

"Stay down on your punches . . . Keep going forward," Don said.

It was time for the second round, and the crowd was cheering loudly. I dominated in the second as well. My entire family was screaming, "Go, Jess!" and "You got this, Jesselyn!" By the third round, we were both tired. I had let in a few punches, but I'd won the match.

When the fight was over, I was pretty pumped. I thought I would be more sore, but I wasn't at all. Afterward Carrie was such a good sport, we hugged and went to the vending machine and bought candy bars. A security guard who'd watched the first round of our match said, "You were both pretty tough out there. Who ended up winning?"

"We were both winners!" Carrie said. I loved that answer. We *were* both winners.

After Fight Night was over, Don took Papi and me to my favorite restaurant, P.F. Chang's, for dinner. I was starving!

Don asked me, "What did you like most about your first fight?"

I smiled. "I liked winning! And I liked that I'm one fight closer to the Junior Olympics."

He laughed. Then he asked, "What did you like least?"

I thought about it for a few seconds and said, "That Mackenzie didn't come to cheer me on."

His voice got soft. "Well, then, I guess you're going to have to tell her she'd better start coming to watch a future boxing champion while there are still tickets available."

That Monday I went to school and told Mackenzie every detail about my first boxing match. She thought it was great! I walked around for weeks after the fight feeling like a new person—literally for weeks.

Dreams and Goals
win my first fight
go to the olympics
win jo nationals

CHAPTER FOUR
WHAT DREAMS ARE MADE OF

Nothing really big ever happened in my hometown of Bergenfield, New Jersey. My father called it the suburbs he'd always dreamed of living in as a kid: tree-lined streets and white picket fences, pretty houses and nice neighbors. There seemed to be a hundred restaurants down Washington Street—everything from Lechón—roasted suckling pig—at one of the many Filipino restaurants, to fish-and-chips at Tommy Fox's Irish pub. But what I loved most were the trains. There always seemed to be a CSX train passing through—on its way to or from New York City. I would imagine what those cars could be carrying . . . clothes, or toys, or millions of Jelly Bellys! The sound of the train horns would go unnoticed once you got used to them, but I hoped I would never get to the point where I didn't hear their whistles blowing.

One time, *Extreme Makeover* came to Bergenfield and redid a house near ours, but after the cameras left, and the episode was long forgotten, the owners ended up having to sell the house because they couldn't pay the increased taxes after the house was all done up. Other than that, things were pretty quiet where I grew up.

To me, Bergenfield had always seemed like a place that needed a bit of shaking up—someone to do something big to put it on the map—so I decided I was going to be that person: the youngest Junior Olympic female gold medalist boxer. I thought that aspiring to be a legend in one's hometown was as good a start as any.

One night at dinner, Papi was explaining to Jesiah that if he wanted to be a boxer like me, he had to take it more seriously. "I *am* taking it seriously!" Jesiah said with a pout. Jesiah had started coming to the gym with me pretty regularly—mostly because Papi made him—but he would only "train" for a bit, then get distracted and go off and play.

"Guess we can't all be passionate about boxing," I said smugly.

"Oh yeah?" Jesiah said defensively. "And *you're* going to the Junior Olympics?"

"Yep," I said, shoveling a spoonful of peas into my mouth.

"Then what?"

His question caught me off guard. I was so focused on training to be ready for a championship at the Junior Olympics that I hadn't really thought about anything beyond that.

Papi looked at me sideways with a curious expression.

"He's got a point," Papi said. "Maybe you should write down some long-term goals for yourself."

★ ★ ★

AFTER DINNER I sat in my bedroom thinking about what exactly I wanted from boxing. What were my goals? I stared at the ceiling for a good long time, because I realized I probably needed a thought-out plan.

My bedroom was my favorite place in the entire house. Everything in my room was soft. Papi had painted the walls white like cotton, which was very soothing to me, and beautiful. I had a desk for studying, and an arts-and-crafts area, a dry-erase board, a comfy mattress with soft pillows, and a fish named Rose who nibbled on my finger. I named Rose after "Thug" Rose Namajunas, the Ultimate

Fighting champion in the strawweight division that year. I think Rose the fish might have been male, but I liked the name and he/she looked like a Rose. And I really, really liked Rose the boxer, because she was tough as nails!

I went over to my desk and pulled out a piece of paper. In the movies they mark off days on regular calendars for regular things to happen, like dance lessons on Tuesday or someone's birthday party coming up. I decided to come up with a calendar for big things that I *wanted* to happen in my life. A calendar of dreams.

My ultimate goal was to be a great boxer someday. But what did that mean, and how was I going to get there?

I had to map it out. So at the top of the piece of paper I wrote "Dream Calendar." Then I quickly drew a twelve-by-twenty grid and started numbering it 1–220. I wanted to fit all 365 days of the year on the paper, but I only got to 220 before I ran out of room. It was a pretty sloppy rough draft.

I thought long and hard about what exactly my goals were going to be. I figured easiest goals to hardest. I went over to my dry-erase board and wrote: "(1) WIN THE REST OF MY MATCHES THIS YEAR" (if Don found me some more girls to fight). Next, I wanted to do at least one state tournament, so I wrote "(2) GOLDEN GLOVES" underneath it. My next goal: "(3) QUALIFY FOR JUNIOR OLYMPICS," which I wrote in big bold letters. I started circling numbers on my dream calendar and would x out numbers after each day I trained toward my goal was completed. Each crossed out number reminded me I was one step closer toward my goals and inspired me to keep going.

The next version of the dream calendar I would make would be full of color and straight lines . . . but something was missing. I still had to figure out what my ultimate goal was. My way-way-in-the-future goal. I thought and thought. Then I thought of my great-grandfather.

Shortly after my first sanctioned fight with Carrie, I visited my great-grandfather in Florida. He was Papi's grandfather, and I always thought it was pretty neat that we had four generations of Silvas still around. Papi's grandfather told me stories of his childhood in Cuba, and he always teased Papi about living in New Jersey, where the winters were so harsh. "When will you see the light and just move down to Florida and enjoy some warmth?" he'd ask.

I was nine years old when Papi's grandpapi woke me up from a sound sleep and said, "Jesselyn, I want you to come with me." It was the middle of the night, and it took my eyes a while to adjust to the light. He handed me a plate of his famous homemade flan—which was this delicious, soft, custardy dessert he'd always make for special occasions—sat me down in the recliner in his small living room, and made me watch hours of boxing matches on cable TV. He knew that I was serious about boxing and wanted to encourage me to follow what I loved. The next night I woke him up to watch boxing on TV. After that it became our evening ritual. During the fights he'd point out what the boxers were doing right and wrong. One night my father came into the room and said, "What are you two doing? It's two a.m.!" Then he got himself a plate of flan and joined us.

Looking back, I think it was some of the best instruction I've ever had.

Not many people knew my great-grandfather was a boxing fan until he found out I had taken up the sport. After that it made our bond tighter until we became almost

inseparable, talking about our favorite fights and boxers and how to improve both mentally and physically. My
great-grandfather was very sick from lung cancer. It felt
like I was just really getting to know him when he started
to get weaker. One time we went to visit him in the hospital
when he was getting chemotherapy. "Jess, I know if you go
pro . . . ," he said through hard breaths, "you'll be having
your first fight in Madison Square Garden." I smiled and
reassured him I'd continue with my boxing career.

He said, "You *will* keep working hard and you *will* be
great. I know that much about you." He was hooked up to
monitors in a hospital room and looked so frail, yet he said
those words with conviction. With a little struggle in his
voice he said, "The day you fight in Madison Square, my
spirit will be there with you. You will see me standing right
there next to you."

I'd never been to the Garden, but I knew it had hosted
thousands of fights, including some of the most famous.
That's where, in 1943, Sugar Ray Robinson fought Henry
Armstrong—two of the greatest boxers in history. They
fought there thirty-seven times combined! Joe Louis fought
there twelve times. In one of the most memorable fights at
the Garden, labeled the Fight of the Century, Muhammad Ali
and Joe Frazier clashed on March 8, 1971, in a heavyweight

championship to end all. Both were undefeated boxers, and both were out for the heavyweight title. Frazier won in fifteen grueling rounds. Then of course there's Mike Tyson's relationship with Madison Square Garden. Spectators loved to come watch the human wrecking ball dominate under that dome—he could sell out the place in minutes. In the 1980s, Tyson was one of the youngest heavyweight champions in history to box in Madison Square Garden, and he's still one of the greatest, most ferocious, and entertaining boxers to watch to this day.

Then there was the important fight between Bernard "the Executioner" Hopkins and Puerto Rican boxer Felix Trinidad on September 29, 2001. Not only did Hopkins become the first man to become the undisputed middleweight champion after defeating Trinidad, but, more importantly, this was the first major sporting event after the September 11 attacks on the World Trade Center and the Pentagon.

But the fight I won't forget wasn't even a main event. In 2017, Mikaela Mayer fought on the undercard of the Vasyl Lomachenko versus Guillermo Rigondeaux fight.

She dominated Nydia Feliciano by a majority decision in four rounds. When you fight undercard, it means you're fighting before the main event—you're the lesser-known boxers.

I had figured out my big dream goal for my dream calendar. I wrote at the very bottom of the dry-erase board in big, big, bold letters:

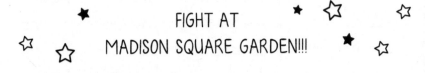

FIGHT AT
MADISON SQUARE GARDEN!!!

But when I fought in the Garden, I decided, I wasn't going to be on the undercard. I was going to headline!

My father is not an emotional man. But when I came down to show him my calendar and tell him about my goals, I could see that he was proud. "This is probably something we should all have," he said. He understood how much boxing meant to me. "Promise me one thing, though, Jesselyn. Don't take shortcuts in life. People think they can cut corners for some things, but it'll always end up taking you more time in the end. Do the hard work. Focus on where you're going."

My father was saying this from experience. When he was in high school, he didn't have any goals. His life wasn't guided. He said he just didn't care about anything. He never even went to prom. He liked football most of all, but not in the way I cared about boxing. He stopped doing his homework. Then he started skipping school and hanging out with the wrong kids. Then he pretty much dropped out of school and life altogether.

When he was sixteen, he ended up in a youth probation program for troubled boys. While in that program he received a surprise letter from his father, who was in prison at the time. In the letter, my grandfather told my father not to make the same bad decisions he had made. He wrote that all bad decisions lead to consequences, and that if my father kept going down that path, he would end up in prison just like him, and that was no life for anybody. And even though the details were a little murky, it was a known fact that Papi's father eventually ended up dead on the streets because of his bad decisions. My father was so moved by this letter that he was determined to focus on making good decisions for himself and his family. A hard life just wasn't going to happen to me if my father had anything to say about it.

I think because of a few hard knocks during his own teenage years, Papi was pretty strict with my brother and me. We had daily chores, and we had firm "Rules of the

Household." Beds were expected to be made in the morning, dishes cleaned and put away at night. We couldn't listen to certain kinds of music, or watch certain shows on TV, no exceptions. There were no sleepovers, and homework had to be done before any playtime happened.

Whenever my father saw us being lazy or fighting with each other, he'd say, "Come on, too much downtime. Get off the couch and go outside!"

I began going to the gym five days a week, several hours a day. Weekends I would usually show up to watch a match or spar with a boy. My technique was improving; my knowledge was expanding. Working with speed bags helped make my shoulders stronger. Sit-ups gave me a tighter core. Being on the treadmill strengthened my calves and improved my breathing. Shadowboxing for hours a week helped with my balance and my arm speed. A person has twenty-seven small bones in each hand. I needed to know my soft spots and how to punch the right way to keep my hands safe. I needed to learn to protect my face and head. I needed to learn to stop dragging my feet. Your brain can be bruised, and concussions heal slowly. I focused on protecting my skull. I punched with my lead hand over and over. I practiced repetitive motion.

I did a full routine every day until I collapsed. My father kept telling me to "use my energy" and fill myself with passion. He would remind me that being passionate about something is better than spending my time watching TV. And I kept dreaming of one day boxing in Madison Square Garden. I was falling in love with boxing, and even if some people thought it was a savage sport, I'd never felt more confident and determined. I was going to accomplish my dreams.

CHAPTER FIVE
SOMETHING LOST,
SOMETHING GAINED

About the same time I created my dream calendar, my father was making his own goals. He quit his night-shift job at the meat processing plant and took a job with shorter day hours as a delivery guy for a Greek restaurant. His stress and chest pains had become so bad that his doctor had recommended trying a lighter load for a while. Switching from the long night job to an easier day job seemed like the logical first step toward change. A career as a food delivery guy wasn't on his dream calendar, but raising two good kids was. He said the most important goal for him was to raise us the right way.

"You kids matter more to me than anything in this whole world," he said. "And you have a chance to do more and be better than any Silva in our family, so, God willing,

I'm going to help you get there." He wanted to be with us more without feeling exhausted all the time, and if that meant sacrificing a better job and a good paycheck, so be it. He was tired of being tired.

With more hours of free time, he began to study to get his GED—which stands for General Education Diploma. Basically, because he had never officially graduated from high school, he had to take this test to get his diploma. He spent a few months cramming for the exam, and received his GED! He told me my dream calendar might be rubbing off on him.

Another goal he had was to get us all eating better and living a healthier lifestyle. He didn't like how often we had takeout or fast food, and said all that was going to have to change. One evening he made us watch a documentary called *What the Health*, which was about our nation's pharmaceutical and meat industries and, in the film-maker's opinion, how bad processed meats are for your body and the environment. It freaked me out so much that after watching the movie, I said, "Forget it! I'm going to be a vegan!"

From that day on I tried to eat a no-animal-product diet. My father and sometimes my brother did too—but we had our "cheat days" . . . which meant we'd eat pizza with lots of cheese, and ice cream for dessert. My father started preparing all-organic lunches with fruit and beans and rice. Never any meat. And we did more research to find the best balanced diet for our new lifestyle. My poor grandmother rolled her eyes when we'd make meals consisting of quinoa and zucchini noodles. "You need some meat in those growing bodies!" she'd say. My father was used to people judging his decisions; it bounced right off him, but sometimes it stuck to me, and I would think about what I was putting into my body more than I wanted to. Truthfully, the fact that there are so many opinions about how people should eat is very confusing. Animals in the wild don't seem to have any problems with their diets.

The problem with boxing—and every boxer experiences this—is the obsession with weight and food that comes with the sport. Weighing a certain amount to fit into a division is part of the game. Papi made sure I didn't obsess about it. He had no intention of raising a girl with an eating disorder. Healthy choices were discussed openly and often in our household. I learned about the benefits of protein, cut the carbs, and made sure I ate plenty of greens and fruits. Thinking about our eating habits was probably the biggest change for our family. A few years earlier we would have had no problem grabbing a quick bite

from the McDonald's drive-thru. What was first a struggle to eat healthier and more consciously became a habit, and now I can't imagine eating the way I used to.

The more time I spent at the gym, the more I got to know my teammates from the Police Athletic League—PAL—gym. They quickly became an extended family to me. There were nine of us altogether—ranging in age from ten to eighteen. I was the only girl, and the youngest, but it didn't seem to bother anybody. When one of them had a rough day at school or at home, we'd help them punch it out in the gym. I saw a few of them go down hard in the ring, and a few of them rise to the top. When one teammate won a big match, we all felt like we'd won—same with losses. I was close with all of them, but Brian and Zack were probably the two I felt the closest to. They were five years older and treated me like a little sister. When I had a bad day, they always knew how to make me laugh.

One of my teammates, nicknamed Flash, landed a top spot fighting in New Jersey's Golden Gloves tournament. Each state had a Golden Gloves tournament, and the winner advanced to nationals. It was a pretty big deal for amateur boxers to advance to that level of fighting. You had to be at least sixteen years old to fight in the Golden Gloves, and no junior-level boxer from our team had ever made it to nationals. Not only was Flash a top boxer representing our team at the national level, but he ended up winning the national title that year! We all felt proud.

But every weekend, as I watched and supported my teammates in match after match, I kept thinking it would be impossible for me to be up there fighting in the Junior Olympics—and definitely not at the Garden—if I didn't have any girls my age to fight and practice on. So I asked Don again if he could get another match together. "I'll see what I can do," he said.

"You haven't forgotten that I want to fight in the Junior Olympics, have you?" I said with a big smile.

"I don't think you'd ever let me forget that," he said and smiled back.

One day while I was doing speed-bag training, Don said he had great news. He had found a girl for me to fight. He'd gotten a call from a coach in New York. The girl might be a bit more experienced, he said, but he thought I could handle her.

We were set to fight at the PAL Show—an event my gym hosted that featured the best amateur boxers in our tri-state area of New York, New Jersey, and Connecticut, and I was going to be one of them! A week before the PAL Show, my father, brother, and I handed out fliers for the event around town. We posted them at school, and in restaurants and shops and dry cleaners. I even brought one to the nail salon where I got my nails painted purple, black, and gold to match my boxing outfit. When Papi delivered food orders, he handed out fliers to customers along with their order. "Come watch my daughter box!" he'd say proudly.

At school, kids seemed interested in learning more about the boxing tournament. They knew I'd been training for bigger matches for a while, but had never asked questions beyond that. It was the first time my classmates seemed genuinely curious about my sport. A bunch of girls asked how I got started, and Mackenzie told them how she'd watched me train. I told them to come to the fight and see for themselves.

My second official sanctioned fight was at 7:00 p.m., Saturday, June 11, 2016. I was now ten years old. This time, it wasn't an away meet like my first match; it was near my hometown at Hackensack High School, and the place was jumping! I admit I was pretty excited to show off a little in front of my friends. Like my first sanctioned fight, it was quite a production: lights, tickets, a photographer, announcers, real referees, and a big boxing ring in the middle of the large gymnasium. I got there early for weigh-in, like all the other fighters.

When I saw the girl I was going to fight, I realized she was much bigger than I'd expected. Her name was Maya, and she was a pretty Puerto Rican with a head of tight braids and defined arm and leg muscles. She was older than me by a year and a half but looked much older.

"Don, how many fights does she have?" I asked.

"Oh, I think eleven or twelve."

Eleven or twelve?! I had only one sanctioned fight.

"That's more than 'a bit more experienced,' Don," Papi said anxiously.

"Jess can handle her."

"How has she found so many girls to fight?" I asked Don.

"She hasn't. She's fought the same two girls half a dozen times. So don't worry."

"But she's still got more experience. I don't know, she might be too strong for Jess." Papi acted like I wasn't even there.

"Papi, I don't care how many fights she has—I want to fight her."

But my father was concerned that fighting a girl with more experience could backfire and cause me to lose my confidence in the ring. Don assured him I'd be fine. He reminded us that boxing isn't just about strength and experience, it's also about agility, stamina, willpower, and smarts. So basically it's a lot like every day of school. I wasn't worried about Maya's experience or her age or her size, because I was going to make up for it with confidence and determination. All I wanted was to achieve my dream of becoming an Olympic gold–winning boxer, and I wasn't going to let someone with a little more experience intimidate me. Plus, with all my hours of training in the gym and sparring with my teammates, I more than made up a few of those fights—at least I hoped so. Okay, so there was a little twinge of doubt, but I pushed it down and didn't give it any attention after that.

"I can handle her," I said to my father.

I weighed in at 72 pounds, but Maya was weighed in at 78 pounds. We didn't need to be exactly the same weight, but we needed to be a few pounds closer before the fight would be allowed to go on. Because it's harder to lose four pounds in thirty minutes than it is to gain, it meant I had to put on four pounds quickly to fight in her division, the 80-pound division. I ate half a sandwich, even though I really wasn't hungry, and drank a bottle of water. It went down too fast, and I got a cramp in my side. It still wasn't enough poundage.

"Get some more water in you. You need more water," Papi said. "And another bite of sandwich."

I pushed away the sandwich. "Papi, stop! I'm going to throw up."

Usually boxers want to lose weight to fight in a lower weight division, but I had been trying to bulk up for this fight for two weeks—while also training hard. The laws of physics, Don had explained to me, apply to boxing: a person who weighs more will land stronger punches. That's why they have weight divisions: lightweight, middleweight, heavyweight. Even the greatest lightweight boxer will find it challenging to win against a middleweighter. So when a boxer determines his or her weight division, they try to weigh at the top of the category. In this fight, I would be on the low end of weight in my division, and Maya would be on the higher end. That meant the laws of physics were against me from the very beginning. But a boxer can't go into a fight thinking about the laws of physics or whether she is on the higher or lower end of her weight division or she'll doom herself. "Someone's gotta be the smaller boxer," Don would say. So it might as well be me this time.

"Three more pounds, just three more pounds," Papi said to me.

"I can't drink any more. I won't be able to move!"

So I put on my whole boxing outfit—including my street shoes.

I just made it. Three pounds' difference. The fight was on!

Before my fight started, I scanned the stands, excited about seeing all my friends from school. I didn't see any of them. Nobody had showed. Not even Mackenzie. Then

I scanned to see if there were any familiar faces from my community—but I saw only my teammates. The only person outside of my boxing crew to come watch me fight was Ms. Nelson, who had been my second-grade teacher. I was glad she had come, but it hurt a little that not one single friend of mine from school made it that day.

Then I saw a group of people waving to me at a VIP table ringside. Papi had purchased special tickets to get that ringside spot to surprise me. Sitting at the table were my uncle and his wife, my brother, and my grandmother. I couldn't believe they all came to watch. It gave me instant confidence.

Before any sanctioned boxing match, boxers have to get their wraps checked by the officials to make sure they're not illegally padded. My great-grandfather once told me that in his day, there was a famous cartoon image of a fighter putting a horseshoe in his boxing glove so he'd be able to get a solid whack on his opponent. He said Jack Dempsey, a well-known boxer in his time, supposedly loaded his glove with a railroad spike when he destroyed Jess Willard in a brutal match in 1919. That of course was way back when, and now the rules are much stricter. In fact, boxers are now given official certified-legal boxing gloves—either a red pair or a blue pair, and that's the color you become for the night. Whenever I'm handed the certified gloves, I think of the image of a horseshoe or a railroad spike tucked away in another boxer's glove somewhere in history.

Nowadays, several referees check equipment and make sure boxers are fighting in the appropriate weight divisions. There are so many last-minute no-shows and changes that it's always a crazy scramble until the actual matches begin. Once in a while you'll hear the announcer say, "Okay, everybody, back to the weigh-in," which means they've had to recalibrate the scales because they were wrong.

It had been seven months since my last sanctioned fight with Carrie in November 2015; I had sparred many boys in between. I was now ten years old, but still fighting in the youth Pee Wee division. I wouldn't move up to the next division, the Bantam division, until I turned eleven. The night I boxed Maya, I was red gloves. My gold, purple, and black boxing outfit was a little tighter on me this time around, since I was growing like a weed; it would probably be the last time I could wear it. We would fight the usual three rounds, one minute each round. Maya was not only way taller, older, and more experienced than I was, but pretty intimidating. She walked around the ring with confidence—maybe it was even arrogance—and with her strong arms and legs flexed. When she saw me enter the ring, she acted all tough, like the lights had just come on and the camera was rolling and it was "showtime." I'd seen this move before. It was just a technique to psyche me out—but it was working. She also had a tough walk, another technique, that made her resemble a wild animal ready to pounce. She wiped her mouth as if she were drooling with hunger. Maybe she was, but so was I. I had learned a thing or two since my first fight, and I had my own set of intimidation tactics. The moment I entered the ring, I was in fighter mode, but I stayed chill. I stared at her hard, assessing her body type. That was *my* intimidation tactic. Never let them see you sweat. Study your opponent. Look them up and down. Don't give too much away. Yes, she might have been a dominating force in the ring, but I had a shot at this. I gave her a hint of the stink eye and lifted my chin to say, *Come on, come get me.* Strong body language is the pride of every boxer.

Headgear on, then the gloves, the mouthpiece last. We both stomped our feet in respect to each judge and went to our corners. Ready. The chanting crowd got me going, and they exploded when Maya and I started to shake our limbs and bounce up and down. My heart was beating out of my chest, but it was more from excitement than nervousness.

Still I had to tell myself to stay balanced and focus. I heard a kid near ringside mock my petite size—"Look at that skinny little girl fighting!" I wasn't going to let it get to me. One of my teammates nudged the guy in the arm and said, "That *skinny little girl* is fierce, bro!"

I closed my eyes and told myself not to doubt who I was or where I came from. The big girl across the ring from me might have been a boxer, but I was a fighter. Fighting was in my DNA. I came from a long line of fighters who had battled tougher situations. I could handle this. I thought of my grandfather and my grandmother and my great-grandfather. I thought of my father and his fight to make it work as a single father juggling work and raising a family. Then I thought of Madison Square Garden and smiled.

The announcer welcomed the match with pomp as he geared up.

He introduced my opponent. A good number of people clapped and cheered. Then he introduced me:

"Annndddd in this corner, from our very own Bergenfield, New Jerseeeyyy, Jesselyn 'Too Cute' Silva!" My teammates and family went nuts with the cheering. I was so glad they had my back.

> **I could handle this.**

Maya and I met in the middle and bumped fists, moved back to our corners, listened to final words from our trainers, and faced the center of the ring, waiting for the bell to signal go time. Once you're in that position, between the ropes, facing your opponent, you're in there and there's no place to hide and no way out after the starting bell rings. So once you're in, you have to be ready to give blood.

Don looked at me and smiled. "Focus on your footwork. Speed is on your side. Show them what you got, Jess."

The bell rang.

Maya came out really hard and got me with one powerful punch. I moved back to adjust. I'd been hit in the face while sparring and during training, but there was always something about that first punch of a new opponent that felt foreign and got my attention. It didn't necessarily hurt, but it was always jarring in the way that anything new takes some getting used to. I needed to adjust to her speed and strength quickly or I'd never make it past round one. I couldn't get off balance. I had to snap with the jab. I concentrated on my breathing and my feet. I had been preparing for this for years, and if I wasn't ready now, I'd never be ready.

"Keep your hands close to your chin," Don was saying.

Papi was hollering, "Jess, jab."

Both Don and Papi were nervous. I could tell because

they were kind of overcoaching, but I didn't mind because I was enjoying the bob and weave of the match. I felt well conditioned and strong. Then I got hit with an uppercut to the jaw—hard. It caught me off guard, and I gave myself a little distance. I shoved my mouthpiece out to my lower lip with my tongue, sucked it back in. Then I moved toward her again.

"That's it, Jess," my teammates were shouting ringside. "You got this, Jess!"

Papi's voice grew louder as the excitement grew: "You're working the wrong hook . . . Half step back . . . Change your angle."

Don threw me some praise: "Yes, Jess, that's it. Hit hard, stay smart."

Maya got in a few more solid uppercuts, throwing me off balance again. I got back in my southpaw stance, jabbing with my right, a few power shots with my left. When I got hit, all I'd think about was trying to get my punch back. *Equal hits and I could actually win this thing*, I thought.

The bell rang.

Round one was over and a win for Maya. But I had kept up with her in dodging hits and had even thrown a few to match hers. I wasn't at all discouraged.

"Jess, you're doing great," Don said. "Just remember to work on your blocking. But you're doing great."

The second and third rounds went pretty much the same as the first. Punch for punch I tried to stay in there, but every once in a while she'd

land a solid blow and I'd have to wait a second to steady myself. While I was adjusting, she'd go in for a body shot. *Thwack!* Body shots stung. I tried to sting back, but I was sore and getting tired. I had never experienced that kind of direct impact. She had me stumbling.

"Gain your feet!" my father called toward the end of the third round.

A right hook, then a cross into my ribs. I knew the round was almost over, but I wasn't sure if I had ten seconds or twenty seconds left, and in boxing, even a few seconds can make all the difference. Ten seconds later the bell for the end of the match rang, and I exhaled. In a flash, it was over. We bumped fists and shook the hands of each other's coaches. Done.

When I came out of the ring, I ripped off my headgear, and my teammates and family started to chant and cheer. Even though I had lost, I had given enough counterpunches and jabs to prove myself a worthy contestant. I had a snarl on my face, and my hair was a wild mess.

"Ha ha!" one of my teammates laughed. "You look like Godzilla!"

"Yeah, and you looked like Godzilla out there boxing, too!" another teammate said.

Don gave me a big squeeze. "She ain't no Godzilla, she's Jesszilla Silva!"

"Jesszilla!" All my teammates laughed. It was true. I had lost, but I had boxed my hardest, and I guess at times I had felt like a beast.

"Good job in there." Don smiled proudly.

"She's a Jesszilla in the ring," said one of my teammates, still laughing.

Don looked at me and said, "Guess you're no longer Jess 'Too Cute' Silva anymore. Looks like you've graduated to being called something a little tougher."

I hadn't thought about it until then, but I had never really wanted to be seen as "too cute" when I boxed. I wanted to be treated the same as any boy, and no little boy boxer would ever be called too cute. I wanted to be the opposite of cute. I wanted to be fierce and feared.

My grandmother came over after the match with a concerned look on her face.

"You know I love you, Jesselyn, but I'm never coming to watch you box again," she said and gave me a great big hug.

She continued, "I simply can't watch you get hurt. But I will always be there in spirit. Okay?"

I gave her a tight hug back and said, "Okay."

I had lost the match, but I also left something behind that night: I left behind people ever seeing me as a boxer who is "Too Cute." I also gained ring experience and one more sanctioned match toward qualifying for the Junior Olympics. With two sanctioned matches now under my belt, and three more to go, I was now more determined than ever to go to the Junior Olympics!

CHAPTER SIX
THE AMAZING INVISIBLE GIRL

My whole body was aching the Monday after the PAL fight, and I had a kink in my back as I lifted myself slowly out of bed that morning. I looked in the mirror and said, "Hello, Jesszilla . . ." It had a good ring to it. Usually after sparring with a teammate at the gym I was a little stiff and crampy, but I wasn't used to the kind of aches and pains that came after a hard match like the one I'd fought on Saturday. Maya's punches had been less predictable than my regular sparring partners', and after coming down from the adrenaline rush of an actual sanctioned fight in front of a large crowd of people, I was completely wiped out. Boxers talk about the post-adrenaline blues, and I was discovering it was a real thing. I felt an overall sense of dullness. I guess after all those crazy stress hormones are done fueling your system for a fight-or-flight situation—fight-or-fight, in my case—everything starts to come down again and your mind feels stalled. That's what was going on with me: inactivity, flat-out exhaustion. It took me longer to recover than I had expected.

I went over to my glittery boxing outfit hanging on my closet door. I took it off the hanger and folded it for the storage bin. I never thought I would grow out of it so quickly. But it didn't matter, because I came to realize I didn't need a fancy outfit to feel like a real boxer. I could wear rags and still be the best out there as long as I was determined and worked hard.

At breakfast Jesiah stuffed two huge bites of banana into each cheek and threatened to explode. I barely touched my food.

"Eh, Jesiah, go finish getting ready for school," Papi said. Jesiah chewed the last of his banana and bounded off to his bedroom. My father could tell something was bothering me.

"You're pretty quiet this morning. You okay?"

"Just sore . . . and it's Monday." I picked at my breakfast.

"Well, try to get some food in you." His eyes were trained on me.

"Papi, is it okay if I skip the gym tonight?"

He paused for a second to process what I'd said, then

smiled. "Yeah, of course. You had a rough fight. Give your muscles a rest."

I was relieved and glad he understood.

We could hear Jesiah knocking things around in his room. He'd crawled under his bed looking for his athletic cup that he wore for football to bring to show-and-tell but was frustrated when he couldn't find it. My father yelled his name. "No banging around," he added.

"I'm looking for my football cup!" Jesiah yelled back.

"Just get ready for school. We don't have any time for horsing around today."

Jesiah responded with a muffled complaint. It had been one of those mornings. Jesiah was grumpy too— Monday mornings weren't his favorite—and my father was busy looking for warm coats because we had woken up to the shock of chilly weather in June. After leaving my untouched breakfast plate, I grabbed a pair of dirty jeans from the hamper, a hoodie that was too small, and socks that didn't match. It was one of those days.

The grumpiness continued on the car ride. My brother and I bickered about every little thing, so my father told us to travel in silence as we listened to cheesy talk radio. We were both ready for school to be out and summer to begin—it had felt like a long school year. Jesiah gave me one last sucker punch "just because," but I was too sore to punch back, so I let him win that one. He stuck out his tongue in victory. I didn't even care.

After we dropped Jesiah off at school, my father twisted sideways in his seat with a look of concern. "What's going on with you today, Jess?"

"Nothing." I stared out the window at Jesiah's school. My brother had joined in a game of tag with a few of his classmates and was making silly faces at one of them as he raced around the playground. Something had been bothering me, but I felt stupid admitting it.

"Are you upset that you lost the fight on Saturday?"

"That's part of it."

"Tell me what else . . . I know something's up with you."

"I don't understand why none of my friends came to watch me box. I mean, I loved that my family was there . . . especially Grandma. But not even Mackenzie showed up. They said they'd come, and they didn't."

"Jesselyn . . ." My father exhaled.

"I know what you're gonna say."

"What?"

" 'That's not what's important.' "

"You're right. That's not what's important. Work hard and focus on your goals—that's what's important. Don't give any of that other stuff one ounce of your energy," he told me.

"But they said they'd be there to cheer me on! And this was important to me."

"You don't need anybody cheering you on, telling you you're good. Don't let that be what drives you. You just need to believe that you're good and challenge yourself to always want to be better. You know you're an amazing girl."

"An amazing invisible girl."

He started to pull away from the curb, but paused to say, "Use this to keep you going. If you want a big crowd, if you want people to see you, keeping pushing for it in the ring."

"You make it sound so easy," I said glumly.

"If it were easy, you wouldn't be doing it."

And with that, he put the car firmly into gear and we both looked ahead at the road.

I knew he was right. He was always right. In fact, Papi always said, "Even when I'm wrong, I'm right." And it was true.

Papi also said that boxing wasn't like other sports because there's "no playing in boxing." He'd say, "You can play football, you can play soccer, but you're not playing when you box." Not only is hitting someone hard work, but so is not getting hit. Hitting someone well and with precision is a craft. A good boxer works on controlling the punch and using the strength of their whole body to punch with

> **You just need to believe that you're good and challenge yourself to always want to be better.**

a lot of power. That isn't playing; it's effort. And I knew I shouldn't worry about who came or didn't come to watch me box.

But there was something else bothering me about that night. It wasn't just that my friends didn't show up; it was that when it was my turn to fight Maya, I felt like we were a separate category of boxers—"the girl boxers"—and it really bothered me when I thought about it. Every time I stepped into the ring, someone was saying, "Be careful out there, little lady," or, "Ohh, the *girl* boxers are going next." It was like we were interrupting their fun or knocking on the door of their clubhouse or something . . . like we were an annoyance. I put in as much time at the gym as the boys on my team, if not more, and yet it always seemed to surprise people when I showed up.

When I first started getting serious about boxing and began mentioning my goal of reaching the Junior Olympics, a woman boxer I met briefly at a gym warned me that people don't like to see girls in the ring punching each other. "No matter how many times we duck under those ropes, it always makes someone feel uncomfortable," she said. "And trust me when I say nobody likes it when they hear a woman say she likes to punch people." But I was too naïve to understand what she meant by it at the time, so I didn't really take her words seriously.

In the film *T-Rex: Her Fight for Gold*, a documentary about Olympic gold–winning boxer Claressa Shields, there's a scene where, after winning the gold medal in the Olympics, a public relations consultant for Team USA tells her she's not going to get sponsors if she keeps telling people she loves "to beat people up and make them cry." Claressa looks the consultant straight in the eye and says, "I box." If a guy had said the same thing, he would have an entire cheering section going wild, and sponsors around the block. But not female boxers. No one knows what to do with female boxers. HBO and Showtime haven't wanted to showcase women's boxing matches, although the tides are turning. Showtime hadn't aired a female boxing match until recently, and HBO just televised a female boxing match for the first time in its forty-five-year history. In May of 2018, thirty-four-year-old Cecilia Braekhus won the welterweight championship against former middleweight champ Kali Reis, and it was a big celebration— not necessarily because of who won or lost, but because a female boxing match was getting recognition on a major television network.

Still, women have work to do to change the way our culture thinks about female boxing. In 2010, the International
Boxing Association made female boxers wear skirts,
because when the women wore shorts, audiences couldn't
tell the difference between male and female boxers until
their headgear was taken off, and they didn't want to be
"deceived." The rules have changed since then—women
can wear shorts again—but despite the progress, it seemed
like other stuff had to change, and I wasn't sure what, or
how to change it.

Me with Olympic
gold-winning boxer
Claressa Shields!

★ ★ ★

AT SCHOOL THAT morning, nobody said anything about my fight. Not one person asked, "How'd you do this weekend?" Mackenzie avoided me altogether. That day my teacher, Ms. Nelson, opened class discussion with an interesting question: Are human lives more important than animal lives? Is a cute little puppy more important in this world than a cute little baby? One of my classmates said, "I would choose the baby, because a person is more important than a dog."

A lot of kids in the classroom started to all talk at once. "Not true!" "Dogs are waayyy nicer than people." "How can you say that?! Dogs are smelly." "I don't like dogs! I like cats." "Yeah, I'm allergic to dogs."

Ms. Nelson then asked, "What about germs? Are people more important than germs?"

A big yes!

"We're always washing germs off our hands, aren't we?" she said. "So germs can't be good, right?"

"Right!" we all said at once.

"But think about it for a moment," Ms. Nelson continued. "Think about the germs that live in your gut. If you chose human life over the life of germs, you wouldn't be around. Your body needs germs to live. There are hundreds of types of bacteria in your belly right now keeping you healthy." It was a weird thing to think about. "Everything has a purpose," she said.

Everything has a purpose. *Everything has a purpose.* That thought rang in my ears. I wondered what the purpose of working so hard to box was. Watching girls get in a ring and punch each other made people uncomfortable. My grandmother would have preferred that I did another sport. So what was the purpose?

Breaking into the "boys only" club? That wasn't originally why I had gone into boxing, but it has become something of a purpose to create equal space for girls and women in this sport as I continue improving and understanding it. When I sparred with boys, I wasn't trying to "beat the boy." I was just trying to belong. Gain their respect. Show them I was part of that world and had every right to be there. But I often felt like they were boxing harder with me to "beat the girl" . . . God forbid they looked bad while sparring with *a girl*! But of course if you were to talk to Papi, he'd say there is no winning and losing in sparring, regardless of whether you're a boy or a girl.

After class, I stopped Mackenzie in the hallway. Her long skinny legs made her the perfect ballerina—her true passion was dancing. She was pulling her fingers nervously through her long black hair. We had known each other a long time, and I knew she played with her hair when she got nervous. I wanted to know why she hadn't showed up to my match.

"Why didn't you come watch me box on Saturday night?" I said. "You knew it was important to me."

She looked down and shuffled her feet. "Um, sorry, Jess. My parents think boxing is too violent. They really didn't want me to go."

"But you watch your brother's football games, and there's tackling and shoving and stuff . . ."

"My dad didn't want me watching you hit people. He said it would make me feel queasy."

"Well, would it?"

"I dunno, Jess . . . He said boxing encourages bad behavior."

Bad behavior? I thought.

"Like it's not a sport that teaches sportsmanship . . . Look at Mike Tyson and all those guys," she continued.

I almost screamed. Mike Tyson is not your typical boxer. He once said, "I try to catch my opponent on the tip of his nose because I try to punch the bone into his brain." So maybe boxing is violent—maybe it's one of the most violent sports around. But I've also seen more compassion and sportsmanship in the ring between fighters than I have on the playground at school. There's a whole lot of respect that goes into a fight. It's not just about hurting people or "the knockout." A boxer might want to break someone down, but there's a silent understanding among boxers that we're all in this together. Sometime after the first sanctioned fight I'd had with the smaller, less experienced girl, Papi had admitted he'd kind of started rooting for her a little! That's just the culture of boxing.

I was disappointed in Mackenzie. "Do you think boxing is just for boys and mean men?"

"No, you know I like that you box. You're doing it for the girls."

I rolled my eyes. Yes and no. I started off doing something I loved, and then it grew in purpose. "Yes . . . I mean, I didn't get into boxing to fight for all of girlkind, but sure, maybe I like representing girls." Except the truth was, I had begun to notice the boy-girl thing everywhere—not just in boxing and in sports but also in certain professions and roles in our culture. Like at the Greek restaurant where my father delivers food, for example; there are no delivery people who are women. Why not? I asked him one day.

"Because they just don't. Because it's not safe for them maybe?"

"But you don't know?"

"I don't know. It's always been men."

And the UPS delivery people, the newspaper carriers,

the presidents of most countries . . . On the other side of things, all the librarians at my school were women, as were most of the teachers, and the nurses at the hospital. Adults kept saying our society was changing, but a good look around said it wasn't.

So if girl boxers made people so uncomfortable that they couldn't even watch, what was my purpose? *Everything has a purpose* . . . I thought back to when I started boxing and all the boys at the gym would say, "Girls don't box," and how for a split second I'd started to believe that maybe they were right. But then I realized that girls *do* box, and they box really well, just as well as boys, sometimes even better. And it's amazing to watch! I thought that maybe everyone else had made us invisible because they didn't know what to do with us. If no one comes to watch, if no one cares to support girl boxers, then in essence, girls don't box because no one sees them doing it.

"I don't get it, Mackenzie. If my best friend won't come watch me box . . ." I stopped midsentence, shrugged in disappointment, and walked away.

After school, Ms. Nelson pulled me aside. "Jess . . . I'm very proud of you. You were wonderful on Saturday!"

"Thank you, Ms. Nelson," I said quietly.

"I was very impressed that you got into that ring. I certainly couldn't do anything like that."

"Yes you could . . . if you set your mind to it."

Ms. Nelson laughed. "I'm learning a lot from you, Jess. I hope you know that."

"You are? But you're the teacher."

"Yes, and on Saturday, you became my teacher. You taught me about real strength and courage."

I smiled and hugged her. It was exactly what I needed to hear.

"They say proper preparation prevents poor performance—the five Ps. Trust the process!" I said proudly, repeating the exact words my coach had told me a few days earlier.

"Well, obviously it's working for you, because you're a very smart young lady," she said. "And a very determined young lady. And I hope you keep fighting." Then she opened her purse. "Here, I got you a little something."

Ms. Nelson handed me a small gift-wrapped box. Inside was a necklace with a *J* and a gold boxing glove with faux diamonds around it.

"For me?" I was completely surprised.

"Do you know how hard it is to find a boxing glove trinket for a necklace?"

Then with a wink she said, "Keep on fighting, Jess, so that in the future

" Girls *do* box. "

it becomes easier to find that kind of charm for other little girl boxers. And you know, with your attitude you're going to get to the Junior Olympics. I just know you will."

"Don't worry, Ms. Nelson. I won't give up."

★ ★ ★

WHEN I GOT home from school that day, a plastic bin waited for me in the kitchen.

"What's this?" I said to Papi.

"It's from the neighbors. They thought you might like it."

I opened the lid of the bin and found dozens of Barbie dolls in a bunch of frozen poses. Some were pristine, but others had knotty hair, and legs and arms that didn't bend properly or were completely missing. One even had permanent purple marker all over her face and body.

We looked at each other and chuckled.

That night, on my soft carpeting, my father, brother, and I played with the Barbies. We weren't very kind to them. Every party turned into a boxing match, and no matter what, it ended with one or more of the Barbies farting and then needing to use the toilet. We laughed hysterically as we mangled their skinny, long limbs together.

Jesiah was holding his side from laughing so hard. "Barbies *are* fun!"

"Barbies are for farting!" I said, which made Jesiah fall over laughing again.

"All right, you clowns, time to clean up and go to bed," said Papi.

My brother and I flung the Barbies we were playing with back into the bin. I looked over at my father, who was on his side, relaxed. He was enjoying this moment with us.

"There are Barbie tennis players and Barbie ice skaters, so why aren't there Barbie boxers?" asked Jesiah.

"Well, boxing isn't one of those sports that people think of first when it comes to girls," said Papi.

"Maybe they need to make a boxing Barbie!" I said, whacking my Barbies together.

"Looks like they already have a couple," Papi said, laughing at the way I was making the dolls wrestle each other dressed in sparkly formal gowns.

When he tucked me in that night, I asked my father if I could talk to him about something. He was always the best listener, and I was lucky I felt comfortable telling my dad anything.

"Papi, I feel like no one is ever going to take me seriously because I'm a girl. No one comes to watch me box. And they all call me the girl boxer, not just, you know, the boxer-boxer . . ."

"Your teammates don't call you the girl boxer. They

get it. They see how hard you work. Plus, fighting for your place in this world builds character. It's part of the journey. Maybe being a girl boxer is way cooler than being a boy boxer because you have to work that much harder to prove yourself."

It was true that my teammates and the coaches at the gym were very supportive of me. They saw how much I trained. I wasn't the little girl coming to throw a few light jabs just to look cute. I loved my teammates for that. Even though they had a bro code, they always included me.

A few weeks after the PAL Night fight, my *abuelo* called from Florida. His cough sounded worse, and his voice sounded weaker. The cancer had spread to other parts of his body, and he was dying.

"The Women's National Golden Gloves is coming up, in Dania Beach," he said. "Not a far drive from my place." He paused to hold back a cough. "Maybe you should come down for it . . . and visit a dying man, too."

I begged Papi to go to Florida, of course to see my great-grandfather, but also for the women's Golden Gloves! My father was hesitant to say yes. It was an expense I didn't think he could afford, but it also seemed like our last opportunity to visit my great-grandfather while he was still alive.

"I know plane tickets are expensive, Papi, so I

understand if we can't go," I said at dinner a few nights later.

"Don't worry about that. Mr. Sweary helped me out."

Mr. Sweary was an interesting story. His name wasn't actually Mr. Sweary; that was just a nickname Papi had given him because he swore a lot. The story of Mr. Sweary had started a few months earlier, when Papi met a woman named Gloria at the gym who was a professional home organizer. Papi laughed when he heard that. "That's a real thing?" he asked.

Gloria explained that it was not only a real thing, but a popular service. "I run a very lucrative business in New York City just organizing people's homes."

"Well, you should hire me," Papi joked. "I have pretty good systems when it comes to organizing my house."

"Really?" She tilted her head in curiosity.

It was true. My father was obsessive about the littlest things. Like, for example, that little space between the counter and stove that no one but Papi cares about. He hated how all the crumbs would constantly get stuck in that one crack. It drove him nuts cleaning it every week. He would go at it with a toothpick and a sponge, but the crumbs would still build up, so he started putting a piece of tin foil in the crack to prevent it from collecting food. Problem solved.

Gloria hired him on the spot!

The next week he was told he would be starting a large organizing project for an important man who didn't have time to organize his home life. Turned out the large job was for a wealthy man who lived in New York City and had a kitchen the size of the gym I box in, and a mouth like a sailor. That was Mr. Sweary.

"Every time he opened his mouth, another curse," my father would say, shaking his head. "I don't know how he motivates anyone with such a potty mouth!" Jesiah and I laughed and laughed at the thought of it.

When Papi got to Mr. Sweary's penthouse apartment, he was shown a room with several boxes.

"Organize these," said Gloria.

"What are 'these'?" Papi asked.

"The family's entire life history in photographs."

"But how can I . . . I don't even know these people."

"Figure it out," Gloria said, and with that, she left the room.

Several brand-new empty photo albums had been left on a bed for him, and Papi spent the entire week piecing together a family's life story just through photographs. He had to judge people's relationships and ages based solely on pictures. Holidays, birthday parties, baby showers, weddings, vacations . . . He put a few thousand photos in their place. Often he'd find a group of photos and have to go back and rearrange an entire year. There were stray photos and people who didn't fit with any particular occasion, but he tried his best to place every image carefully throughout.

"What a life!" he said one night after a long day at Mr. Sweary's. I wasn't sure if he was talking about our life or Mr. Sweary's.

At the end of the week, Papi got paid a good sum of money for his work. Soon after, we were headed to Florida to make our own family memories. I packed a camera.

CHAPTER SEVEN
HOW I SPENT SUMMER VACATION

Every Sunday, my grandma took Jesiah and me to the Chapel, thirty minutes away in Wayne, New Jersey. It's a Spanish-speaking Christian church with a Bible school that Jesiah and I also went to twice a week. My grandma had known the pastor there since before I was born, and it had become her community and her sanctuary over time. Papi never came with us—he wasn't religious, but he was a man of faith. He always said, "Anything that causes division cannot be God. God is love and God is peace." So Papi did not go to church with us. My grandmother stopped chastising him about it a long time ago—but they did have an unspoken agreement about her taking us every Sunday. Jesiah and I never . . . ever . . . missed Sunday church with our grandmother. I didn't mind spending the extra time with her. She was always gentle and kind with us. And she was beautiful, too. Wherever we went, people would compliment her on her youthful skin and good looks. Spending time with her, even if it was at church, made up some of my favorite memories.

I hated going to church when I was younger, though. I remember shuffling around in the pew with nervous energy and never listening to anything the minister said. Sermons were boring and confusing—I didn't get how grown-ups could make sense of any of it. One hour in church seemed like a week.

"I'd rather go to the dentist," Jesiah would say.

"I'd rather stand in front of a dartboard," I would say back, and he would laugh.

But as I got older, I started to listen more. I began to like hearing the stories in Spanish, and the music coming from the choir, and I got to know a bunch of cool kids.

On the Sunday morning before we left for Florida to see Abuelo, my grandmother said a prayer out loud: "Please, God, let my granddaughter outgrow her obsession with this boxing thing." Then she looked at me to see if I was listening. I rolled my eyes. "And if she won't listen to her wise old grandmother, then please keep her safe in the boxing ring."

As we walked out of church later that morning, she said, "I don't understand why you're traveling all the way down to Florida to watch a boxing tournament instead of spending quality time with your great-grandfather. Why don't you go to the beach?" We usually didn't tell my grandmother about boxing tournaments because she tended to worry too much. But my grandmother always found out about them anyway, because Jesiah always spilled the beans.

"Grandma, we'll go to the beach, too."

She gave me a look that said she didn't really believe me.

"But I also want to see a little of this." And I began to shadowbox as we walked down the street.

"Oh, this fighting you do, Jess . . . I don't like it. It makes me nervous. It's not a sport for young ladies."

"Grandma! That's such an old-fashioned thing to say."

"It's old-fashioned to say girls shouldn't hit people?"

"Yeah. People don't talk that way anymore."

"Well then, tell me, how do people talk these days?"

"You know, like how girls can do anything boys can do, and girl power and that kind of stuff."

"Oh, all you girls with your ideas of women's liberation. Let me tell you, it isn't easy working and raising children." She looked at my blank expression. "You'll understand when you're older."

"*You* worked and raised children," I said to her.

"Yes, and it wasn't easy! See these gray hairs? Do you

remember Ms. Lopez across the street from us? She never married or had children and died with a full head of raven-black hair. And not a wrinkle on her face! You children are hard work."

"Yeah, well, she probably died of loneliness."

My grandmother laughed heartily.

I remember Papi telling us stories about how Grandma struggled to balance raising her three sons and working to provide the things they needed the best way she could. When she arrived in the United States from Ecuador at age seventeen, she enrolled in high school and sold clothing on the street to pay for her tiny one-bedroom apartment while she managed to raise her first son all by herself. She was determined to learn English fluently, and spent many late hours learning how to read in English. She knew if she never learned the language, she would never make it in this country. Many days she slept only a few hours before heading to her next job, and other days she'd go without much to eat. It wasn't easy for my grandmother, and when I thought about her story more, I was in awe of her strength and determination. I also felt a little guilty and privileged for the life I took for granted.

The next morning, we left for Florida and I promised my grandmother I'd spend plenty of time swimming in the ocean.

"Is this the Specific Ocean?" Jesiah said, his face pressed against the airplane window.

"It's *Pacific* Ocean, and no, it's the Atlantic," I said.

We had been on an airplane a few times before to visit my family in Florida, and every time, Jesiah and I would squeeze our heads together and look out the window at all the mazes and shapes of little and big towns below and wonder who all those people were.

"Just passing by . . . ," Jesiah would say, and wave.

There were so many people living different lives and telling different stories.

The pretty woman across the aisle asked if we were heading down to Florida for vacation. I said we were heading down to watch the Women's National Golden Gloves tournament.

I always loved to see people's reactions when I told them I boxed.

"You mean like kickboxing?" she said.

"No, boxing, fighting, ring, boxer," I responded proudly.

"Oh, sounds rough. Probably different than male boxing?" the woman asked.

A lot of times people asked me if I thought women fought differently from men. "Yes and no," I'd say. Women punched just as hard, and were just as good with their footwork and speed, strength, and agility—all the things

that men boxers were good at—but women were different in that their passion came from a different place. I
could never explain it fully, but it was true. I usually said,
"Because we females have to work harder than men." What
I didn't say is that we work harder because we've got to feel
like we belong.

"Why did you pick up boxing as a sport?" the nice
woman on the plane asked. She seemed genuinely curious.

"Because she likes to punch people," Jesiah said with a
snicker.

"Especially you!" I wrestled him in his seat.

I quickly changed the subject, because I hated answer-
ing that question. Boxing for me had gotten past the point
of explaining it as "just really fun!" It was something
beyond that, but it was hard to put into words. Yes, it was
my passion, and yes, I saw it as a lifelong love, but would
people understand that coming from a girl? Sometimes I
wondered.

When we saw my great-grandfather, he looked frail
and sickly. But the minute he saw us in the airport, he lit
up. "Come, come give your abuelo a hug!"

I loved being at my great-grandfather's place in Florida.
I especially liked to cook with him. Before my great-
grandmother died, he never cooked. But when she got sick,
he started doing the cooking to care for her and nourish

her. He cooked out of love. His secret ingredient to everything he made: love.

We played cards and talked about boxing a lot, too. My father asked him if going to the Golden Gloves might be too much for him, and he said he wouldn't miss it for the world!

"I won't make it to see Jesselyn fight in a Golden Gloves, so I might as well go with you tomorrow and imagine her there."

I hadn't expected the Women's National Golden Gloves event to be so huge! It was like I'd left Earth and landed on another planet. There were women fighters everywhere—four hundred female boxers, to be exact—from all parts of the country. In my regular life, it was impossible to find women fighting at all, and here I was in the center of something enormous! There were women from as far away as California, and women of all ages.

The Golden Gloves started in 1927. It's the biggest amateur boxing tournament in the United States. But until the 1990s, it was only for men.

Many of the female boxers I met had other jobs—really cool jobs like police officer, teen counselor, and military officer. One boxer was a guard for a high-security prison. Another worked for the New York City bomb squad. Several boxers I met were training to go from elite amateur to professional boxer. These women! Where had they been all my life!

The fights were hard-core, and the punches they delivered were explosive. I couldn't take it all in fast enough. They fought three two-minute rounds scored by five judges, and I tried to learn their moves and study their strategies as much as possible. Toward the final matches I heard one boxer yell from the ring, "I am here and I deserve to be here!" I thought, *Yes!* Another time I overheard a boxer being interviewed and she said, "You hear the guys saying, 'Oh, women can't make it in this sport . . .' Well, you gotta answer back somehow!" Yes again! These were my people! I think I understood for the first time what women were talking about when they referred to girl power, because it was all right here in this arena.

Toward the end of the day, we were walking around and Papi was getting anxious about keeping Jesiah from running off. My great-grandpa was always teaching me things.

"Did you know that Muhammad Ali won his first Golden Gloves at age fourteen?" he said.

"Really? He was that young?"

"Of course, now you can't even compete in the Golden Gloves until you're sixteen . . ."

Right as my great-grandfather was saying this, I kid you not, Laila Ali—*the* Laila Ali—passed by us.

"Jesselyn, go over and introduce yourself," my great-grandfather said.

"No way!"

"Ohhh, don't be silly. Take it from a wise old man—don't let any opportunity pass you by. She crossed your path—*your* path—for a reason. Embrace it!"

It did feel like fate, and she was larger than life! (Truly, I didn't expect her to be so tall.)

I jogged over to her. "Can I take a photo with you?" I asked a little sheepishly.

"Of course!" she said. She hugged me in the photo and told me to never give up.

First time meeting Laila Ali

"Ms. Ali," I asked.

"Yes?"

"Why do you box?"

She laughed. "I box to feel free," she said. Her smile relaxed.

That was such a good answer, I thought. *I should start saying that.*

It was the truest answer I had heard about my sport. I box to feel free. It wasn't just about punching people. It was about feeling something deeper. I loved the way it felt to move in the ring, make my opponent miss and land a solid hit. What I loved most was the release of energy and the feeling of strength boxing gave me. It felt so good to feel strong! And to be able to do it with skill, strength, control, and discipline . . . That's freedom. Some people think freedom means being a little out of control or without limits, like when you go exploring in the woods alone. But for me freedom was to be completely in control in a tight space with an opponent rushing toward me.

I loved the way it felt to overcome the things I didn't like to do. I didn't like to run. In fact, I hated the treadmill. Running two miles during training was at one time torture for me . . . but now it's not so bad. Some days I even look forward to running.

My brother started giving me the business after Laila Ali walked away. Teasing me and jabbing at me. So I threw a few jabs back.

"Hey, you've got good form," a man passing by said.

"Oh, thanks."

"Are you a boxer?"

"Yeah, I box," I said with fake modesty.

"Can I see a few more moves?"

I showed him some of my moves—a backhand hook, shoulder slip, duck under, a little bob and weave.

"Very nice. You need a little help with your footwork. Where are you from?"

"Bergenfield, New Jersey," I told him.

"I'm right across the river in New York. My name is Carl."

Carl was a gray-haired, middle-aged Puerto Rican man. He was strong and in good shape, and you could just tell by the way he spoke and carried himself that he was probably a strict coach.

We shook hands.

"I'm training for the Junior Olympics," I said proudly.

"Well that would be quite an accomplishment if you got there. Who are you working with now?" he asked.

"Don Somerville."

"Oh really? Don's a great guy . . . You're more than welcome to come to my gym. You ask him, okay? Tell Don you met me and I'd like to work with you."

Turns out Carl was a head coach for the women's boxing team at the New York Athletic Club—one of the nicest, fanciest clubs in New York City.

"You coach women?!" I asked.

"Yes, three or four at a time."

"Wow! I've never met a boxing coach who trains that many women at once."

"Well, now you have. Jess, you've got some really good moves. Would you consider training with me for the summer at the NYAC?"

"Really?!"

I couldn't believe my ears! I could already imagine writing my summer essay for school. It would begin "'My Summer Vacation' by Jesselyn Silva. I spent my entire summer training with Carl, an elite coach at the New York Athletic Club. *The* New York Athletic Club. I worked out and sparred with top athletes by day and dined on the finest meals by night . . ."

"Well, hang on a second," said my father cautiously.

My summer essay came to a screeching halt. I knew there would be a "hang on a second" somewhere in there.

"It's gonna be kinda hard to swing it, you know . . ." my father said.

"Yes, I understand it would be a big commitment for you," Carl said. "I'll coach her for free for the summer"—he looked at me—"if you promise to work really hard and be serious about it."

We exchanged numbers and he said, "I see a spark in you, Jess. Not all boxers have it, but you do. Think about training with me." He walked away. I was so happy to meet a coach who worked with women!

"Papi, please can we, can we *please*?!"

"I don't think so, Jess. How am I gonna get you to the city, and Jesiah, and work . . . Besides, you know how those gyms are. I just wanna know their real agenda. Are they trying to help or do they just want to cash in?"

It was true. The boxing world was messed up that way. A lot of the well-known gyms are just out to produce the biggest names in boxing—and they start them young. I'd heard of coaches buying kids cars and equipment, clothes, watches, phones, whatever to get them to commit to their gym. They tell them they're great, that they're the best, but it's all about the reputation of the gym. Then they use them up and spit them out if they don't make the cut.

Abuelo chimed in, "Oh, Pedrito, don't overthink it. Give Jesselyn the opportunity of a lifetime. These kinds of things only come around once—take it from a wise old man."

It was a deal! I would begin training with Carl in the summertime.

That night my great-grandfather barely touched his food.

"Abuelo, are you feeling okay?" I asked.

"I knew the Golden Gloves would be too much for you," said Papi.

"No, no, it was wonderful! Being around all those strong women, Jess. It was good for you to experience it. Such talent in those women. You have given an old man a day to remember."

★ ★ ★

IT'S IMPOSSIBLE TO find parking near Central Park, where the New York Athletic Club is. We had made a deal that I would train with Carl in the summertime on heavy foot-work but still continue training at the PAL with Don. We finally found a parking spot several blocks away. My father complained the entire walk to the gym that he was going to get a parking ticket anyway and he should have sucked it up and paid for a parking garage. "But forty-five dollars for a couple hours of parking? That's crazy. I'm not paying that!"

When we got to the front door of the athletic club, a very large, very muscular man in a doorman's uniform stopped us. "No suit, no entry," he said to my father, holding out his hand firmly.

"What do you mean, no suit, no entry. We're going to the gym."

"Yeah, there's a dress code."

"For the gym?!"

"To enter the building." He showed us the dress code explaining the rules.

GENTLEMEN—Jackets are optional in most areas. Slacks, a collared shirt and dress shoes are permitted. Shirts must be tucked in. Jackets are required in the Main Dining Room and Cocktail Lounge.

LADIES—Permitted attire refers to business suits, tailored pant or skirt ensembles, and dresses. Spandex, open midriffs, halter tops, leggings, denim and extremely short hemlines (more than 3" above the knee, as a guideline) are not permitted.

JEANS, T-SHIRTS, SNEAKERS AND FLIP-FLOPS ARE PROHIBITED.

Jesiah thought it was hysterical that you had to get dressed up to go inside a place to dress down into sweats.

"Listen, we don't have formal clothes with us. My daughter is a boxer, and she was invited here by one of your trainers to use your gym."

"Name of the trainer?" the doorman said matter-of-factly.

"Carl."

"Last name?"

Papi stumbled for a bit . . . He couldn't remember Carl's last name.

"One moment, please," the doorman said with a sigh.

The doorman went inside and made a phone call. When he came out, he said, "Are you Jesselyn?"

"Yes," I mumbled, a bit intimidated by the situation.

"You? You were invited to train here? You must be pretty talented, because I've never seen someone so young train here before."

He told us we could enter through the back entrance near the dumpsters and take the service elevator.

"This is cool! It's like a bat cave!" Jesiah said.

The New York Athletic Club was large! Large fancy and large huge. I'd known it was going to be nice, but I'd never thought it would be so over-the-top. It offered everything a boxer could need and want and more. This was no little gym, like the kind I was used to. No sweaty-sock smell or rubbed-raw boxing mats or splintery gym floors or mop-water-smelling locker rooms. It smelled like fresh laundry in the locker room and chlorine in the hallways. The boxing gym was on the seventh floor—to get there you traveled up an elevator past several other gyms specific to individual sports. The swimming pool (and sauna and whirlpool tub) were on one floor; and a running track, full-size basketball court, cardio equipment, and weights were on another. Squash and racquetball courts were on almost every floor, and there was a wellness center and physical therapy floor, handball, and a dojo floor, as well as wrestling and fencing in the basement. This place was unreal! And I was going to be training here! Then the elevator rang at the seventh floor. I couldn't believe my eyes: it was the fanciest, most state-of-the-art boxing facility I'd ever seen. "Spotless!" my father said. And it was. It was as if not one drop of sweat had ever hit the floor. Two boxing rings, tons of heavy and speed bags, plus anything you could ask for as far as strength and endurance equipment . . . They

had it all. They even had central AC! Not one creaky fan in the place. Some of the places I boxed in didn't even have fans.

"Olympic medalists train here," Papi said, "so of course they're gonna have AC."

We all laughed.

"It feels like Christmas!" I said.

"You're never gonna wanna leave," said Jesiah, who was busy touching everything.

"This is just for the summer, Jess, so don't get too pie in the sky," Papi said. "But make it count, you know?"

"How much do you think it costs to be a member here?" I asked him.

"Very, very expensive. Nothing that I could afford."

Jesiah and I both said, "Ohhhhhhh" at the same time.

My father then explained that unlike other gyms, you can't just pay online and be a member or anything like that. You have to get invited to be a member—then you have to interview with board members, and get accepted like it's some sort of college. I kind of didn't like that part of it because it didn't seem very welcoming; in my other gyms, no one ever needed an invitation to join. But this one was really, really swanky!

Little did I expect that it would be such a grueling

summer—I trained with Carl three days a week and we focused solely on footwork, which is his specialty. He placed cones in a line and I jumped over them. Again. And again. And . . . again. His workouts were some of the toughest conditioning I'd ever experienced. My body ached. Muscles I never knew I had ached. Even my head ached. But man, my leg muscles got strong.

Carl said, "One reason a lot of boxers lose fights is that they don't have strong enough legs for a long fight. I've seen guys out there collapse in the third round not from a punch but because they couldn't support their shaking muscles any longer."

So we kept training until fatigue set in, and then we'd train more.

"You're not going to lose on a standing eight-count because of your own exhaustion, okay, Jess?"

Between huffs and puffs, I said okay.

An eight-count is like a knockdown without really being knocked down. In amateur boxing, a ref calls an eight-count if he or she notices a boxer being hit with several hard shots. In some cases, an eight-count can be given after even just one power punch. It depends on the ref.

We worked on balance drills, and I focused on blocking and staying upright. I studied boxing moves, focused on stance and balance, strengthened my footwork, and

> **Boxing, in that sense, is a game of inches, and every inch counts.**

practiced learning how to read my opponents better. We worked on combinations and the angles of my punches over and over and over again. And when I was finished doing a full day with Carl, I'd wake up the next day and do a full workout with Don.

Their coaching styles were different. Carl was quieter and concentrated on movement, footwork, and getting inside your opponent. Don was loud and pushed his fighters to use their reach, to keep their distance, to work the opponent from the outside. Getting inside your opponent means you get as close to them as you can without getting knocked around, and it is critical for a boxer to know how to get inside and be able to do it well, because it not only allows a fighter to stay on top of their opponent, but puts them in close range to get solid and more accurate hits. You also have to be able to adjust as a boxer, so being able to defend from the outside is just as important, because it allows a fighter to keep their opponent away through jabs and straight punches. Boxing, in that sense, is a game of inches, and every inch counts.

It might sound confusing to some people, but having knowledge in both areas of working a fighter from mental strength and physical strength is really important for a boxer.

As the summer came to a close, I knew I wasn't going to return to work with Carl, and it was a bittersweet feeling. Bitter because I loved working with Carl and I would miss him and everyone I had met there. Everybody at the New York Athletic Club was genuine and helpful and made me feel like I belonged there. Sweet because it was getting too hard for Papi to get me there all the time—and even harder to find parking! And yes, he did get a ticket on the first day. During the third week, his car got towed because he parked too close to a fire hydrant. In New York City you can't be closer than fifteen feet, and Papi was about a foot shy of that. When he asked a taxi driver where they took cars when they towed them in New York City, the driver said, "It's your lucky day . . . I'm on my lunch break and will take you there for free." But it wasn't Papi's lucky day, because it cost us three hundred dollars to get our car back. A few weeks after the towing incident, we got into a minor car accident on the way home from the club. As he exchanged insurance information with the sweet lady who had bumped into us, he said, "I'm *done* with New York!"

"I'm done with New York too," I told Papi. "But it was worth it!" I smiled.

Carl called a month after school started. "Hi, Jesselyn, how are you doing?"

I loved hearing his voice again. "Hi, Carl!" I was genuinely surprised he had called.

"There's a group of fighters coming all the way from Ireland . . . and . . ."

"And?" I said with excitement and anticipation.

He laughed. "There's a girl your age . . . Well, she's a little older, but she doesn't have as much experience under her belt as you do. I think you'd be an even match. You interested?"

Was I interested?! I jumped for joy!

CHAPTER EIGHT
WHEN YOUR FEET STOP MOVING,
TROUBLE STARTS

The fight with the Irish girl was a last-minute thing. Carl told me about it on a Friday, and I was weighing in on Saturday. It was at the famous Gleason's Gym in Brooklyn, New York. People call Gleason's the Cathedral of Boxing because not only is it the oldest and most popular boxing gym in the world, but they're known for churning out top-ranked contenders, especially in the Irish fight scene. It's kind of like a museum when you walk in: photos of fighters everywhere and trophies and memorabilia and funny signs like the one in bold letters that says "No smoking or spitting on the floor." To fight at Gleason's? Saying it was an honor was an understatement.

I hadn't trained with Carl since the summer, and it

was a chilly October morning when I walked through the door and first spotted my opponent. I felt ready . . . until I saw the girl. Her name was Lorraine, and she was much taller and older than I expected, and much, much bigger. She had this beautiful, thick, sandy-blond hair, fair skin, a strong body, and a wild look in her eye.

"Are you nervous, Papi?"

"No, why would you say that?"

I giggled at the sweat on his shirt.

As you enter the gym, there's a big yellow sign on the wall with a quote by the poet Virgil: "Now, whoever has courage and a strong and collected spirit in his breast let him come forward, lace on the gloves and put up his hands." Courage and a collected spirit in my breast . . . Carl came over to me as I was studying the quote on the wall.

"What do you think of Virgil's words?" he asked me.

"They're okay, but it would be better if it said courage in *her* breast! Next time I'm here, I'll bring a black Sharpie and make a few edits."

He laughed. "I have a feeling you're going to do all right today."

I was secretly very nervous, but didn't show it, mostly because I didn't want to worry Papi.

The two teams fighting each other were New York

Metro versus Ireland. I was fighting for Metro. The Irish team had come all the way from Ireland just to box. For some reason, that made me really nervous. If she'd flown all the way from Ireland to fight an American girl, Lorraine must be pretty serious.

A familiar voice behind me called my name. It was a boxer named Sylvie I'd met in Florida a few months earlier at the Golden Gloves tournament. She's Puerto Rican with a great Southern accent, and really tall with long brown hair and brown eyes.

"You boxing that one?" She pointed to the tall Irish girl.

"Yeah, and I'm kinda freaking out."

"Naw . . . don't worry about size. It's all in the training, and I know you got some skills. Besides, Carl wouldn't have brought you here if he didn't think you could handle it."

She made me feel a little better.

During weigh-in, Lorraine came in at ten pounds heavier than me. You can shed a few pounds or put on a few pounds thirty minutes before a fight, but you can't gain or lose ten.

"She came in over over over!" I said to Papi and Carl. "But I really want to fight her. She's come all the way from Ireland. Please?"

"Jess, it looks like we'll have to forfeit the fight," Papi said.

"No! I want to do this. Carl, is there anything we can do?"

"You can fight as an exhibition, but it won't count as a sanctioned fight," he said. That was okay with me, and it was fine with her.

People have said that each boxing match tells its own story. I thought of that every time I entered the ring. It's a story told through body language. What was my story going to be that day? The day I met Lorraine, I didn't know what to expect. I could hear her club members huddled around each other with their thick Irish accents, and I thought of my immigrant grandparents with their thick accents. I thought about their stories and their fights.

Well, as the saying goes, you can't judge a book by its cover. Lorraine might have been much older and much bigger, but the fight only went two rounds. Her size didn't matter: I dominated her. The additional footwork training from Carl really helped. In the first round, I knocked her around pretty hard and she started to cry. In the second round she lost in a technical knockout. We didn't bother going a third round. That was the end of it. I was happy it went only two rounds—the girl didn't have that much experience, and it was no fun beating up someone who didn't have the right kind of training. She was pretty cool, though. Afterward we talked about boxing and Ireland and then got a candy bar.

Coach and me after the
match at Gleason's

My Gleason's
trophy

★ ★ ★

SOMETHING CHANGED IN me after the boxing match that
night at Gleason's. Maybe because it was an easy win, or
maybe it was because all my hard work was paying off.
Maybe because of the inspiring words of Virgil I felt like I
was now carrying "a strong and collected spirit" in myself.

I didn't know, but I began to approach boxing a little differently, more passionately than ever. I was now in fifth grade and in a few months I would turn eleven and move up to the 11–12 Bantam boxing division. This would be a more competitive division. The girls participating would be more experienced, and it had the potential to draw in more female opponents . . . at least that's what I hoped. So I made a promise to myself that I would train harder and focus on my craft. I was in the gym five or six days a week, two to three hours a day. I sparred boy after boy and once in a blue moon I would spar a girl. I even got another sanctioned match with a girl from New York—I defeated her easily in three rounds, which got me one match closer to the five sanctioned matches needed for the Junior Olympics. But there was something else I started to notice as I got older. Even though I was still laser focused on making it to the Junior Olympics, I thought less about needing to take on sanctioned fights with girls to get my numbers up and more on sparring with people, usually boys, who were more experienced than I was. I figured if I really wanted to compete at a higher level, I couldn't just sit around and wait for sanctioned fights to happen—I needed to spar tougher competitors, and a lot of them. I thought less about my wins and losses, and more on my development. I began to notice my entire self changing. I don't mean just the normal "developing" stuff that adults always want to "discuss" (eww!). My body was getting stronger. Muscles that most kids my age didn't even have were becoming more defined. My hand speed increased, my power punches were much harder, and my footwork was quicker. Boxing not only helped my body's reflexes, but somehow, if there is such a thing, also helped my mind's reflexes and timing. Hitting and ducking came more naturally now, and I wasn't trying so hard to get the moves down. I just boxed. In boxing they call that having rhythm—when your timing happens and things start to click. It's also when you've gained the skills needed to sur-vive in the ring. I had learned how to have patience to set something up before a punch. Most people don't know it, but boxing really is a thinking sport. And I had learned to think like a fighter. Why? How? I guess because when you get so many hands laid on you, you learn to fend. It became automatic, like being on cruise control. Don once said that boxers are like drummers the way their arms use their sticks to get the rhythm down through muscle memory, and that to get the actions down in your brain, you have to start young. This was no spare-time sport—it required memory, like learning another language. It was constant

(or track, depending on weather) . . . (which I
hate!)
Light stretching of legs
Solo boxing drills
3 rounds of shadowboxing
Put gloves on—6 rounds of bag work
(work on something different each round)
3 rounds of mitt work with Don
After boxing, work on conditioning
Another 1 1/2 miles of running . . .
(which I hate even more!!)
10 sets of 8 push-ups
4 sets of 25 sit-ups
6 sets of 4 pull-ups
4 sets of 20 leg raises
Proper hydration . . .

I had come a long way since the first time I curiously
put on those smelly boxing gloves at age seven and felt a bit
tougher. Now I felt fierce.

★ ★ ★

WHEN I FIRST started boxing in sanctioned matches at age
nine, I got noticed by a local newspaper reporter who was

covering one of my teammate's matches and ended up interviewing me. My boxing story and my goal to one day fight in the Junior Olympics got me a front-page story in the newspaper—with my picture in it and everything. A few kids were even talking about it at school. That's when I started to get a reputation as a fighter, and maybe that made me a little too confident.

DANIELLE PARHIZKARAN/STAFF PHOTOGRAPHER

Jesselyn Silva, 9, working on her footwork with coach Don Somerville at a gym in Hackensack.

Boxer's biggest fight is finding opponents

Bergenfield girl shows rare dedication

One afternoon in the fall of sixth grade, Papi picked me up at school. I got in the car and jokingly said to my father that I wanted to beat some boy up for mouthing off in class all the time. "Jess, I want to talk with you about something," he said. He had a look of concern on his face. I couldn't begin to imagine what he was about to say.

"Training to box is a skill you're building. It's not meant to be used anywhere but inside the ring. But if anyone puts their hands on you, you've got to be able to defend your-self. As long as you're not initiating it."

"I know, Papi. I was just kidding . . ."

"Do you understand what I'm saying? I don't want to see you throwing any punches but those between the ropes unprovoked. You got that?"

"Yeah."

I knew what he was talking about. He had told me sto-ries about when he was a kid and got into fights, and how one bad decision and hanging out with the wrong people can lead to other, bigger bad decisions. "Stay in your lane," he often said. I made a promise to him and to myself that I would never, ever use my boxing skills outside the gym.

But I broke that promise.

At recess one day a few weeks after the conversation I had in the car with Papi, a bunch of us sixth graders were playing football. It was mostly boys—not too many other girls liked to play football, but I did. The quarterback threw me a long pass to win the game, and I caught it for a touchdown. This kid went to grab my legs and missed me. I danced around and did a little cheer; maybe I celebrated a bit too much. Then one of the boys on the other team tried to push me down. But as he lunged toward me, I dodged, and he fell to the ground. Everyone started to laugh at him. Even I laughed at him, and then I even stuck out my tongue and said, "Nice try."

He was clearly embarrassed . . . and furious. "Why do you always have to act so tough?" he said.

"Because I am tough." I was feeling smug.

Later, in the classroom, the same boy approached me and said, "You think you're better than everyone else just because you box and because you got some articles written about you . . . Why can't you act like a normal girl."

I am a normal girl, I thought. Then I was angry.

He egged me on. "I bet you're not as tough as you think you are." I should have known better than to take the bait, but without even thinking, I pushed him in the chest. And I guess I pushed him really hard, because he fell backward into the bookshelf with a loud crash and all the books fell on top of him.

"Kids, kids!" Our teacher rushed over. "This is completely unacceptable behavior! Jess, I'm very surprised by this. Both of you, down to the principal's office immediately."

We both got detention for a week.

I told my father the news when he picked me up from school that day and he was upset.

"Detention?!" he said when he had me alone in the car. "This means you're missing training at the gym today. And you will miss training all week."

"I'm sor—"

"This doesn't sound like something you'd do, Jess. I'm really surprised."

"I didn't mean to . . ."

"You keep going down this path and you might as well forget about boxing altogether." My father never lost his temper, but he was angry. "I'm not going to waste my time and your brother's time getting you to the gym if you're going to use your boxing skills to be a troublemaker," he continued.

"Papi, please! I'm sorry. He just said some things that really upset me."

"I've told you a million times, don't give negativity any energy. That was a test of your mental strength, and you failed. You need to be tougher next time—not physically, mentally. I don't want you to walk around like a tough guy just because you know some boxing moves. You hear me?"

"Yes. I hear you."

I had failed. I knew I had failed. But what I didn't tell Papi was that "toughness" is a weird thing for girls. Boys can be tough all they want—the tougher the better—but girls can only be so tough before people think they're just trying to "act better than everyone else" or they're "weird" and it's no longer acceptable. It was really confusing, this girl power thing.

Papi ended up grounding me for several days. I sat at home, in my bedroom, staring at my dream calendar, and was completely miserable. Three days felt like an eternity. Being away from the gym was torture. But as luck would have it, Don called to tell us he had finally arranged a fight against a twelve-year-old girl from Rhode Island. Papi accepted the match.

"Papi, you need to let me train! I can't go into a fight without training."

He knew this was important to me. "Fine. But no more fighting at school."

When I saw Don at the gym three days later, I was ready

to get back to work. It might sound crazy, but when I didn't train, even just for a few days, I felt awful.

"Listen," Don said to me. "Sometimes when people know you're a boxer, they're gonna want to get at you . . . you know . . . try to see what you've got. Turn the other cheek and don't be easily provoked. You read me?"

"Yes, totally," I said.

"Good. We've missed you at the gym . . ." I looked down at the gym floor I loved and knew so well. I felt a little silly thinking about pushing the boy at school.

"Hey—we've all been there," Don said. "And let me tell you something many of us have learned the hard way. When your feet stop moving, trouble happens. You know what I'm saying?"

"Yes."

"So let's get back to it. You have a fight to win."

Don had warned me that the girl I was going to fight was really good and I needed to be prepared for a tough match. I was definitely more concerned than I had been about other opponents, yet, with all the training I'd done with Carl and Don, maybe I had a shot.

The sanctioned match was another PAL fight, so I was on my home turf. Even so, the moment I laid eyes on her, I knew this wasn't going to be an easy match. Her name was Lindsay, and she was a year older than me. She was also bigger, taller, more experienced, and physically stronger. Papi looked nervous. "Man," he said, "you can see her muscles . . . they're so defined." It was true. The girl was cut. But I liked that about her. She had been working hard at her craft and took the sport seriously.

Before the fight, a professional photographer came over to us and said, "Hey, can I get a photograph of you two?"

"Sure!" Lindsay said, smiling. We put our arms around each other and posed like we were best friends. The photographer looked through his camera, scratched his chin and said, "No, not like that . . . Maybe a little tougher." So we posed tougher. "No . . . not that either. Why don't you two face each other and do a face-off photo." So we turned to each other. I stared her straight in the eye like I meant business. Then we laughed.

After that, we focused on the match.

Right before the fight, Papi went over to the DJ, who was playing songs the boxers could walk in to, and handed him a CD.

"Can you play this for my daughter Jesselyn Silva's entrance?" he asked.

"Does it have swears in it?"

"Nope, it's all positive."

"Sure, man."

Jesiah decided to join the fun and asked if he could walk me to the ring. "Of course!" I was surprised and delighted. The music that introduced me started to play. It was one of my uncle's songs that he had written and composed called "It's My Job." Papi's brother was an incredible musician and had been creating inspirational music for a long time. This particular song was very special to me.

Go hard, go hard
I'm gonna go hard
Gonna go hard
Like it's my job
Like it's my job
I'm gonna go hard
Gonna go hard
Like it's my job
Like it's my job
We family, can't you see
The resemblance, we all made from God
We all made from God!

And to have Jesiah walking me to the ring, and my coach behind me rubbing my shoulders and supporting me with encouraging words . . . it just blew me away. I put my hands on my little brother's shoulders and started to strut. It was Jesszilla time! If I was going to fight Lindsay from Rhode Island, at least I would do it with flair!

★ ★ ★

I COULD TELL the minute the first bell rang that I was in trouble, because she came out with speed, balance, and strong punches. But I was committed to working hard for that fight.

"Jess, inside work, inside work," I heard Don yelling.

Then he started to call out the names of punches and combos he wanted me to throw.

"Lunchtime!" he said, so I threw a straight left to her stomach.

Every coach has their own special names for punches. It's like a code coaches use to tell their boxers which punches to throw when they're in the ring so the opponent doesn't know what's coming next—kind of like when a catcher signals to the pitcher in baseball.

"Half-step Diego," he would call out, and I'd throw an uppercut. This punch was named in memory of the famous boxer Diego Corrales, who was a multi-time world champion fighter in two divisions. He was honored with the

Fight of the Year in 2005 for his bout with José Castillo, in which Corrales was knocked down in the tenth round. The Fight of the Year award is voted on by a number of boxing organizations and institutions for the very best, most exciting fight that year. It was given to Corrales in 2005 because somehow Corrales beat the count and got back to his feet with one black eye. Seconds later, Castillo knocked down Corrales again, but he got back up with two black eyes. Barely able to see, Corrales managed to connect the perfect left-hand hook and pushed Castillo against the ropes. Without mercy, Corrales finished him by landing several punches in a row, knocking Castillo out and causing the ref to stop the fight. It was the best fight of the year and one for the books. But exactly two years later, Corrales was killed in a motorcycle accident, pronounced dead at the scene. His legacy lives on. And I think of his amazing comeback fight every time Don calls for a "half-step Diego."

We have a number of other code names. My favorite: "puppy ears."

I will say that many code words were used during this fight as we each tried to get the upper hand. And we were switching moves around on the fly to get any advantage, because when you're fighting a bigger girl, you gotta adjust. It's never comfortable getting closer to something that could really hurt you, but the only way to score points in these situations is to become an inside fighter. Apparently I wasn't doing that very well. But I was working very hard that round.

"Come on, stop fighting at arm's length," Don was yelling. "Jess!" Yelling louder.

Don wasn't the kind of coach who got mad easily, unless you weren't listening. But he was a loud coach, he was a passionate coach, and he liked to yell. He liked to show what he was capable of doing as a coach, but he reserved screaming for when it was absolutely necessary. That day it was necessary. Round one was over, and it had been a disaster. I'd been thrown around badly.

"Don't get off the game plan. Get your head back in it."

I spat water into the bucket. "I can beat her."

"I know you can. She's throwing her punches fast, so slow her down by working off your feint. Work the ring and your combinations. Don't let her dictate the fight."

"Okay . . ." The bell rang for round two.

I thought about the combinations I had worked on over and over again. I got in with several one-two-five-twos (jab-cross-left-uppercut-cross) and knocked her off balance.

"Yeah, Jess! Again!"

So again with a combination. I had picked up so many moves in the previous several months of training that they were working themselves. Round two was mine.

When the bell for round three rang, I came in hard and fast and got a little overly confident.

"Come on, girl!" I said to her. And threw a punch that barely hit her.

"That's all you got?" she said.

We were both tired toward the end, but she put on the pressure. She handed me some big hooks. Even the ref grimaced. A couple twos missed her, and I ended up pulling back. I looked at Don and he was clapping to show his support . . . but I felt like I could have done more. After the fight I was furious with myself. I didn't even care this time that it was one more sanctioned fight closer to the Junior Olympics. I wanted to win. Maybe if I had trained harder, maybe if I hadn't taken three days off right before the fight . . . maybe . . . maybe . . .

I had learned my lesson about fighting outside the ring, and I had gained a deeper respect for what's done inside it. The boxing ring, that beautiful square, had become my wild country. It's where I would roam. It's where I could blaze a trail and learn about myself. When I was outside that space, I would put on my street clothes and go back to being a kid. I thought again about that quote from Virgil that I had read at Gleason's: "Now, whoever has courage and a strong and collected spirit in his breast let him come forward, lace on the gloves and put up his hands."

A strong and collected spirit. Maybe that's what power is about. It isn't about using it whenever you want, it's keeping a collected spirit and using strength when it's most needed.

I stared at my dream calendar during the days I was grounded. It had changed several times since my first draft. I had made it more colorful and neater, but my goals were mostly the same:

WIN MY FIRST MATCH
   (which I did)
FIGHT IN GOLDEN GLOVES
   (going to happen when I'm able to
   at age sixteen!)
QUALIFY FOR JUNIOR OLYMPICS
   (yet to be determined)
WIN JUNIOR OLYMPICS
   (yet to be determined)
(LOTS OF BLANK SPACES FOR MORE
   GOALS HERE . . .)

FIGHT AT MADISON SQUARE GARDEN
(will happen someday!)

I made a new goal on my dream calendar after the fight with the Rhode Island girl—one I would probably work at my entire life. It read:

BE A BETTER ME!

CHAPTER NINE
SAVING FACE

Around the time I lost to Lindsay from Rhode Island, I began to notice that my approach to boxing was changing even more—or maybe my mind-set was changing. Whatever it was, something about the sport felt different to me. It wasn't instant, like a light bulb going on and off; it was more a kind of force that I could feel building from within. When I first started to box, Papi and I would joke that I was whacking at the bag to "get my crazies out." But lately I had been thinking that that wasn't why I boxed anymore. The things that got me into the ring in the first place—it looked fun, I liked punching people—still got me motivated, but what I'd begun to like most about boxing wasn't about the hitting or even that I was getting into a ring to fight; it was that when I boxed, no one else could enter the ring with me to fight for me. It was just me against my opponent in there, sweating it out. It was mine to win and it was mine to lose. Instead of getting my crazies out, I was thinking about getting inside myself more and how to get inside my opponent. It's what happens as your skills as a boxer improve—instead of it being just a physical sport, it becomes a deeply mental one.

I wanted to fuel my strengths in other ways. I continued to train harder and stay focused and use boxing as my outlet for whatever was going on outside the ring, but I also wanted to figure out how I was going to be a better me. I decided the best place to begin was to look at my bad habits. In the ring I had a few bad habits, like not moving my head enough and dropping my lead hand at times, and I wasn't good at getting inside my opponents yet.

Other bad habits I wanted to correct were biting my nails, not making my bed in the morning, forgetting to say my prayers at night, not doing my homework, forgetting stuff at school, and, my worst offense, according to Papi, leaving the rubber bands for my braces on the kitchen table. Those were the first bad habits that came to mind. I figured if I could break some bad habits, if I could let go of the bad stuff, I could make more space for good habits and clear my mind of the negative that sometimes invaded my thoughts.

Good and bad habits aside, the only true way to get really good at boxing was to focus on my craft daily. So I increased my hours at the gym. I sparred with my teammates, my coaches, friends of teammates, visiting boxers at the gym, anyone willing to get in the ring for some technical sparring. I hungered for fights, and Don went looking.

Working the
speed bag →

← Sparring

One day he told me he had arranged a fight for me in Paterson, New Jersey, with a girl from Philly named Cassidy. She would be one of the toughest competitors I'd faced yet, because her record was 6-0 and she had a reputation for being strong and scrappy.

Cassidy weighed five pounds more than me at weigh-in, but it was close enough to count as a sanctioned fight. She was tall and lean with long, slinky arms, and she glared at me with a look of determination. I really liked that, because it upped my game. We were both there to win, and we were going to challenge each other. I couldn't wait to get into the ring . . . Of course, Papi was pacing back and forth. The anticipation grew as our hands were wrapped and our coaches gave us final words of advice. Don said to me, "With a fighter like this, everything is going to happen really quickly. There's a lot you're going to be taking in all at once. Just focus on what you've learned. Stay relaxed and have fun."

"And protect your face," Papi interrupted.

"Yes, protect your face," Don said. "This girl is coming into this match with confidence—she hasn't lost yet. Let's see if you can be the first to beat her."

Papi added, "She might have a record of 6-0, but it doesn't mean anything, you know?"

"After this match, she'll know what it feels like to lose," I said with confidence.

As the three of us continued our prefight talk, I noticed my mom and members of her side of the family walk into the gym, including my half sister, who was four years old. It was my mom's first time watching me fight, along with my aunt and a little cousin. They all lived near Paterson, so it made sense that they would show up, especially since my dad had mentioned the fight to my mom. And the reason Papi had mentioned it to her was that she was planning to be with us that weekend. I guess seeing her there made me both a little nervous and really excited, because all of a sudden my heart started to beat out of my chest. *Focus, Jess, focus*, I thought. I was dying to show my mom my skills. I wanted to win more than anything now!

Just before the match started, I walked over and said hi to her. My mother hugged me and wished me luck, and told me to kick some butt. Then she gave Jesiah a great big hug and spun him around. I was glad she was there.

I always thought it was cool to see my mom and dad in the same room together. They were really nice to each other—it wasn't weird or awkward like in some families. And when I would ask Papi why he doesn't look for another woman to marry, he would just say, "Naw, I have no time for marriage. I don't want that for us—at least not in the 'I do,' ring-on-the-finger sort of way . . . Besides, what do you need a stepmom for when you've got your mother? Just because she only visits on the weekends doesn't mean you've got any less of a mother." It was very true, and I needed to be reminded of that.

The fight started quickly after the announcer introduced us, and Cassidy came in fast. But I was going to bring the fight to her, and I came in just as hard. We were both landing our shots, and neither of us were backing down. It was a solid first round, and there was some aggressive punching on full display.

The thirty-second bell rang and Don called "alpha time." In boxing, your coach will call out a code word or phrase to

POW!

indicate that there's thirty seconds left on the clock. It tells the boxer they need to use every ounce of energy they have left. Before each match, Don and I would come up with a code phrase. In the last fight it was "Be different!" this time, "alpha time."

"Come on, Jess, no time to waste," I heard Papi yell.

"Extra push, extra push!" called Don.

"Give it your all!" Papi said.

Family members chanted, "Go, Jesszilla!"

Time goes by quickly when you're watching someone else fight, but when you're in the ring, especially in those last thirty seconds of a round, time moves slowly. Every hit, every move matters.

In those last few seconds, I landed some pretty hard punches on Cassidy and could hear my mother cheering for me. I thought, *Yaaayyyy, I like this feeling*. So I landed another and another. I could hear my father say, "Let's go, Jess," and Don say, "Pick up your hands," and before I knew it, the bell had rung and the round was over. Because I'd gotten a late start in the round, I couldn't tell if I'd won or lost, but I knew I'd ended it solidly and that my opponent knew I meant business.

"Okay, you're doing well keeping up with her, but you need to move your head and get inside of her more," said Don.

I took a swig of water. "Okay."

"And you're dropping your hands. Gotta keep them up."

"Okay, pick up my hands," I said.

The bell rang for round two and I busted out. I threw some of my hardest punches at her, and for every four I landed, she landed one.

I had the hometown advantage, and the crowd was definitely on my side. Every time I landed a solid punch, the gym cheered and I thought, *Yes! I want to do that again and get the crowd cheering more!*

I counterpunched and got out of range of her hits more quickly.

In the second round I came out with force and even got an eight-count on her. "I'm coming for you!" I said with a fierceness I was learning to enjoy.

By the third round I had gotten the advantage, waited for her, got inside of her, struck hard, and before I knew it, the fight was over.

All three rounds had been a solid battle. Our bodies were heaving and bruised. The judges' decision on who had won would be close. I was pretty sure I would come out victorious. But you never know how they're gonna score a fight.

Cassidy and I stood in the center of the ring with the ref, waiting for the results . . . The win went to . . . "the red

corner." The Philly girl had won? Even Cassidy was surprised. I could hear my family screaming. There was still
clapping for Cassidy, but the crowd was questioning why
the blue corner hadn't won. "I don't know!" a person in
the crowd said loudly. "Jess was robbed!"

"No way, judges!" Papi's brother yelled. "Come on—
you're kidding, right? Jess was the clear winner!"

Don was upset and started to question the judges'
decision. "Our opponent got an eight-count the second
round!" He said. But their decision was made.

After the match, I was given a second-place medal but I
was so angry at not winning that I threw it on the ground.
Don yelled at me. "Hey, my boxers don't act like that. Pick
up your medal and always remember it's not a loss, it's a
lesson." My mother was disappointed that I didn't get the
decision. Everyone was disappointed.
And I was disappointed not only
because I had lost, but because I had
really wanted to show my mom how
strong I was. Later she would tell me
she already knew how strong I was
and also how proud she is to have me
as a daughter . . . but it would have
been nice to land the win anyway.

> **It's not
> a loss,
> it's a
> lesson.**

I had never seen Don and my father so upset. The decision was split two to one, and the ref said to my father afterward, "I really thought your daughter won." But scoring a fight is a weird thing. You'd think it would be easy and straightforward, but it's one of the most flawed things about boxing. The way it's supposed to work is that judges score by the number of punches thrown. If you get knocked down, you lose a point. Sometimes they use a ten-point system in amateur boxing—which is the same system they use in professional boxing. Yet boxers get robbed by the judges all the time, especially if you have a home-court advantage.

Judges are looking for hard, clean punches when you fight. Defense is just as important—how solidly a boxer is slipping, parrying, and blocking shots, whether you're controlling the ring and enforcing your will and style. But many boxers have had some pretty bad decisions called on matches they clearly won.

Don walked over to the girl's coach and talked to him calmly. When he was finished talking, the coaches shook hands and Don came back to our raucous group.

"Listen. There's a show in Long Branch, New Jersey, tomorrow. The girl's coach said she would stay another day and fight you in a rematch."

"Yes!" I said.

"Well, wait . . . hold up," said Papi. "You're okay for back-to-back fights?"

"Papi—I want to beat this girl . . . I *did* beat this girl. I want to prove it. I'm not even tired!"

It was settled. A rematch on Sunday. A chance for redemption.

The next morning I was a bit sore and felt disorganized, but I was more ready than I had been the previous day. Usually I packed my gym bag the night before a match, but I was so focused on the rematch and rattled by the loss on Saturday that I forgot to get everything together. One of my lucky socks was missing, and I couldn't find any hair ties, but fortunately my dad always kept spare hair ties in the car. We got there . . . and it turned out that our rematch was the first fight of the day. "Good!" my dad said. He wouldn't have to go through the anxiety of waiting.

The weigh-in went smoothly, and I shook Cassidy's hand firmly then walked away without saying a word. Usually I was fine with talking to my opponents, but that day I had come to take care of business. Also, I could tell Cassidy was on cloud nine from the victory she had stolen from me the day before. I knew she thought it was going to be a cakewalk: get in and get out. But it was not going to go her way today! The girl just looked way too confident. I was pretty calm, and ready for the rematch. Don hadn't shown up yet, and I started to wonder if he was okay. He was never late. Then Papi delivered the bad news. "Don just called . . . He forgot he has to attend his nephew's birthday party today, and his wife isn't letting him out of it." My eyes went wide. I hadn't fought a match without Don in my corner in a very long time. "But Joe and Mark are here, and they'll coach you through it." Joe and Mark were coaches from my gym, but truthfully, it didn't matter who was coaching me that day: I had come to win. I had come for blood. I wasn't going to lose. My ego had been bruised the day before. Not today. I'd dominate every round so the judges would have no choice but to give me the decision.

But as I was getting ready to enter the ring, I realized I had forgotten my headgear. And I completely panicked.

"Papi!" I said as I dug through my bag just to double-check. "I didn't pack my headgear."

I thought he was going to flip his lid—he was the most orderly person, and hated when things didn't go smoothly.

"Jess," he said, trying not to seem upset. "Where do you think you left it?"

"I think I left it at yesterday's match."

I had been so furious about the decision that I didn't even remember packing up my stuff to leave. I was sure it was still there, sitting on some bench.

"Don't worry about it; we'll find someone else's you can borrow."

I could always rely on my father.

I raced around looking for anyone I knew, and luckily found a couple of teammates who were fighting that day. "Hey, Brian, can I borrow your headgear?"

"My headgear?"

"Yeah. I'm the first match and I forgot to pack it."

"Yeah, sure, Jess, but it ain't gonna fit."

"I don't care—I need something!"

"Okay. Good luck, Jesszilla." With that, he handed me his headgear, but just looking at it, I knew it was going to be way too big.

Papi and I quickly adjusted the Velcro, but even at its tightest, it was too large. I was worried the refs weren't going to let me fight, so I turned my one ponytail into two buns and shoved them in to try to get it even tighter.

Papi shook his head. "Let's hope this works . . ."

Just as I was heading to the ring, I noticed a familiar face smiling and waving at me. It was Mackenzie and her father. She had come! I exhaled, gave her a huge smile and waved back.

As I stepped into the ring, it felt surreal, like I was floating, like I was on another level that day. There was a big crowd and lots of cheering on either side. Since we were the first fight of the day, people weren't yet tired of watching match after match. All eyes were on us.

At the start of round one, I came out big and loud with my body. I was there to make a statement, and I did. Truthfully, round one wasn't even a fight. I completely dominated, and by the time the bell rang, I knew I was going to be victorious.

But then in the second round, I went in too hard with a punch and strained my left biceps. I couldn't let the judges see how hurt I was, so I pushed through it. But the pain was strong by the end of the round. Again, I came out on top. This one was mine.

I iced my arm for twenty seconds and was back in the ring to finish her, which I did with every ounce of strength I had in my body. I won in a unanimous decision by the judges.

I had enough sanctioned fights under my belt to

compete in the Junior Olympics. Now all I had to do was win at regionals. I would train even harder.

Resting between rounds

Championship belt

★ ★ ★

AS MY FATHER tucked me in that night, I said, "Papi, I read in a library book that in the early days—"

"You mean when I was a kid?" he said jokingly.

"No, like when those old-fashioned cars were around."

"So maybe you're thinking of the early 1900s?"

"Yeah, then."

"Okay, go on."

"I read that in the early 1900s, the three most popular sports in the United States were baseball, horse racing, and boxing."

"That sounds about right," Papi said.

"Baseball is still popular," I said, carefully studying my father's reaction.

"Yes."

"I guess horse racing is still popular—especially that race where all the ladies wear fancy hats."

"The Kentucky Derby."

"Yeah. It looks stupid, but people like it."

"That's because people like to gamble their money on it," he said.

"And at one time, boxing was more popular than baseball."

"Yeah . . . It was more popular. Because boxing is known to be the most difficult sport in the world."

"The book said that boxing has lost its popularity over the years and that if you compare boxing with football or baseball, those sports have a lot more fans—and more well-known players—than boxing."

"Well, I can see how that's true."

"Why?"

"Think about it. In football or baseball, there are one or two major playoff games or world series, and many of the players are known and have huge followings because of the state the team plays for. Boxing started with eight world championships, and now it's grown to seventeen weight classes and four boxing organizations sanctioning fights. It's harder to keep track of the boxers, and yes, the big championships are on late at night or you have to pay sixty dollars to watch it on pay-per-view . . ."

My father said his theory is that boxing has lost popularity because of bad judging and corruption.

"I just think it's messed up, Papi. You don't have to pay to watch the Super Bowl."

"Well, I guess the point is, maybe the sport isn't less popular; it just needs some fresh faces to get people interested in it so that championships aren't on in the middle of the night."

I said, "That's me! I'm going to be that fresh face! I'm gonna be the next Laila Ali or Claressa Shields! I'm gonna bring boxing's popularity back."

"If you want change, be the change."

"Hmm. Maybe I need a sponsor like Everlast or Under Armour," I said, thinking out loud.

Papi hooted laughter. "Maybe you should just think about going to sleep."

"If I had a sponsor like all the greats, I'd make girl boxing really popular!"

I jumped out of bed and ran over to my dream calendar. In purple Sharpie I wrote, "GET A SPONSOR!"

"I like your thinking!" Papi said.

In the boxing world, it's hard for women to get sponsors. It's all about image, and nobody wants to represent a bloodthirsty woman. So it was like that: without sponsors and coverage, women were left unseen more than seen. And in my opinion, that seemed bad for the sport of boxing.

CHAPTER TEN
GROWING A THICK SKIN

B y now everyone in school knew me as the girl boxer. It might have had something to do with the local newspaper and television coverage that began to appear about my boxing journey and my desire to compete in the Junior Olympics. Mostly kids thought my goals were pretty cool. Sometimes it was the adults who had problems with it.

By now, at age twelve, I was receiving a lot of media coverage about my boxing career—and particularly about my goal of winning the Junior Olympics. Then an article about me appeared in a newspaper with worldwide readership. I made the mistake of scrolling through the readers' comments on the newspaper's website. There were many positive remarks: "Jess, you're awesome! Keep up the hard work." And "I think she'll bring change to a sport that isn't well understood. Go, Jesszilla!" But there were many negative comments as well. Like this one: "How can her parents expose her to such a violent sport at such a young age!" And "She doesn't have any opponents to box because boxing for young kids is dangerous." Another person commented, "She'll break her pretty nose and be done with it." *Ouch!* I thought. *What kind of a person would write such a thing?* And actually, I have the perfect nose for boxing. It's flat enough not to bleed. I've never once gotten a bloody nose from fighting. (Knock on wood.) I've seen noses explode plenty of times—some boxers just have those kinds of noses; one tap in just the right spot, and it's a gusher. Sometimes I've even been the one doing the exploding.

"Stop reading the comments!" Papi told me. "You're always going to have critics in this sport, no matter if you're a male or female. Boxing just always carries this shadow with it. So don't fuel it." Then he paused. "In fact," he continued, "you're always going to have critics in your life, not just in boxing, so my advice is to grow a thick skin."

"What does that mean?" I asked.

"*Grow a thick skin* is an expression that means don't get upset when people have opinions about you or criticize you in any way. Because at the end of the day, they're only just opinions and they don't matter."

Soon after the article appeared, which was when I

was in sixth grade, I was in art class, my favorite subject in school, when I got some criticism from my art teacher. Art class was always on Monday, and usually I was glad to start the week that way. I loved to draw, especially super-heroes . . . and Captain Underpants for Jesiah. I didn't like to draw flowers or horses or balloons like some of the other girls. I don't think my art teacher was thrilled that I was always drawing Spider-Man.

"It's for my teammate Brian. He loves Spider-Man!"

"Maybe something else this week."

"Why?"

"Because you are a talented artist and drawing many things will develop your skills."

Along with being a boxer, I had a reputation for being a pretty good artist—at least that's what my art teacher said. A few years ago, our school had a fire safety poster drawing contest and my "Hear the Beep When you Sleep" poster won second place.

This wasn't the first time my art teacher had encouraged me to develop my talents. It also wasn't the first time she suggested I draw something other than superhe-  roes . . . I knew what she was get-ting at, so I pulled out a blank sheet of paper and drew a beach landscape. It actually wasn't half bad. I made really good waves rolling along a shoreline, some birds in the sky, and a bright sun. I looked at it and it was pretty. To complete the picture, I drew Superman flying in the sky.

My art teacher looked at the drawing and shook her head.

After class, I helped gather homework for Mackenzie, who had recently hurt her ankle when she fell down some stairs and was on crutches.

My middle school was big—three floors big. So big that it even had an elevator, but you could only use it if you were injured or had a disability. It was so awesome helping Mackenzie around for that week, because we got to use the elevator and could be late to all our classes. After art class, she and I were late for science and rode up and down the elevator, laughing, until a teacher told us to get to class.

On our way to science I told her about an upcoming sparring match I had with a boy at the gym.

"You like this kid?"

"What do you mean? Yeah, he's my friend."

"No, I mean like-like."

"No way! Do I look like an adult to be thinking that way? Gross! He's like a brother to me. Yuck!"

"Why do you always have to box boys?"

"Because there aren't a lot of girls to box. If more girls boxed, then I'd be sparring with girls."

I was always trying to explain to my friends at school that boxing was as much of an art form and a sport as any of their hobbies. Blood, sweat, and tears were my fists of ink. My ducks and dodges on the mat were like any dance move.

We entered the science classroom, and all eyes turned to us.

"Glad you got here, ladies," our science teacher said. "Mackenzie, I hope your leg is feeling better. Go get your bridges at the back counter."

In science class, the challenge that week had been to make a bridge out of exactly one hundred Popsicle sticks and a bottle of Elmer's Glue. Mine was not the best bridge project in the class. It was a little crooked and a lot wobbly, but it was good enough to hold the weight of a few books placed on top. That was the challenge: build a bridge that could support as much weight as possible.

Everyone had approached the challenge differently. Some bridges didn't have much support on top. Others had crossing bars or V-supports—very impressive. Mine was flat on the bottom and held twenty-seven textbooks. The winner's held sixty-eight. It was pretty amazing to see sixty-eight textbooks balance on a little bridge made of Popsicle sticks.

"Hey." A boy in my class leaned over.

I looked at him weirdly.

"Pretty cool of you."

"What is," I said.

"To sign up for the wrestling team."

Mackenzie looked at me and said, "Say what?"

"I figured why not . . . Wasn't like I was going to get the lead in the school play."

"Why do you always do these crazy sports," she said, trying to balance another book on her very wobbly Popsicle-stick bridge.

"I wanted to try it."

"But why wrestling?"

"I don't know. I guess I like combat sports."

I'd tried football briefly, but I'd seen how big the boys were in football and said no thanks. So I'd signed up for the wrestling team. There were five other girls besides me, but otherwise it was all boys. I didn't know a single thing about wrestling, and it was totally different from boxing. But I figured it would help with my endurance since wrestling has longer matches and involves more grappling and full-body contact.

"Are you gonna wrestle boys?" Mackenzie asked, still with a confused look on her face.

"Yep."

"What does your father think?"

"Well, I haven't told him yet."

"That should be an interesting conversation."

★ ★ ★

"HOW'D THE BRIDGE project turn out today in class?"

"I got it to hold twenty-seven books."

"That's pretty good!"

"But I wanted to get more."

"Yeah, well, maybe use Krazy Glue instead of Elmer's next time."

We both laughed.

"Oh, Papi, just to let you know, I've signed up for wrestling."

"Wrestling?!" Papi was cutting carrots for that night's salad. "Oh, that's cool, but don't you think you should stick to boxing?"

"I can do both—and wrestling will help me stay in shape. It's three days a week right after school."

"Well, I have a feeling you won't take no for an answer."

"Probably not."

That night, my father looked tired as he sat at his desk paying bills.

"Papi . . . thanks for believing in me." I gave him a big hug.

"Always, Jess."

"Why, though? Why do you do so much for us?"

"Because . . ." He closed his checkbook. "You know, I've got one shot at raising you and Jesiah, and I'm going to do it the best that I can. I'm gonna make mistakes because I'm learning the same as you're learning. But I'm still gonna try my best."

I knew that he had sacrificed a lot over the years to raise Jesiah and me—taking a job he didn't really like, completely changing his lifestyle—but we were so lucky to have him.

"So what is a new goal for you, Jess, besides wrestling? What is something you really want to do?"

> **I want to help create a world where there's no boy and girl stereotypes . . . Especially when it comes to sports.**

I thought about that question for a beat. I'd actually been thinking about the answer for a while.

"I want to help create a world where there's no boy or girl stereotypes . . . Especially when it comes to sports. It's just boxers boxing and wrestlers wrestling and gymnasts being gymnasts."

Just then, my dad's cell phone rang. Papi and I

looked at each other, surprised. No one ever called us this late at night.

At first, Papi didn't answer the phone, expecting to hear bad news, because the number on the screen belonged to a cousin of his he hadn't spoken to in a really long time. He knew what the call was about. But he finally answered the phone.

"Hello? Oh hey, Pedro Antonio," my father said. (I told you there are a lot of Pedros in my family . . .)

It was about my great-grandfather. Papi left the room saying "Mmm-hmm" a lot. A few minutes later he came back into the room. "Jess, Abuelo has died."

I burst into tears. Even though he was old and we all knew he was going to die, it was still a shock. I was never, ever going to see him again or hear his voice or watch old boxing matches with him, or eat his spicy food. I could barely wrap my mind around it. When we were down in Florida visiting him the previous summer, he'd said to me, "You know, Jess, the great thing about dying is that you only get to do it once.

"And . . . ," he had continued with his usual gentleness, "the same is true about living, so make your life worth living."

CHAPTER ELEVEN
PLAYIN' NO GAMES

It was almost the end of my sixth-grade year and I was fighting in the regional tournament for the Junior Olympics, which was held once in the summer and once in the winter. This was the summer tournament—my first actual tournament—and it was 92 degrees in the shade that day as my father and I looped around the block searching for parking. The regional tournament was held at the Police Athletic League Center in Yonkers, New York, which was at one time an armory building that looked like a fortress from another time period. Finally, we found an open space. I got out with my gym bag as Papi loaded the meter with quarters. With the last quarter inserted we were set to walk away when the meter suddenly flashed red: "Out of Order."

"Out of order?!" Papi fumed as he rattled the meter. "I want my quarters back!" But that wasn't going to happen. A man walking past us said, "It's Yonkers—what do you expect?" A working parking meter for one thing. We got back in the car and circled until finally we found a parking garage ten blocks away.

Outside the Police Athletic League, boys in heavy sweatpants were jumping rope in the hot sun to shed a pound or two before weigh-in. There was an air of anxiety as we walked through the large gates surrounding the gym. I'd sparred plenty, and boxed in several matches, but tournaments were different—more fighters, tougher competition, more stress. Like in matches, boxers move up and down in weight divisions all the time, so you never know who you'll box until the day you arrive. I was fighting a girl named Molly who was ten years old and from New York. I was two years older. She was a slender white girl with French braids and a pretty voice. Even though Molly was younger and had less experience, boxing is one of those sports where you just never know what will happen. A few hard punches can change everything. Don always said be confident, be smart, and make sure you always have fun in there—a steady balance. Whoever won this match would move on to the national championship tournament in West Virginia. This one fight was a big deal. If I won here, I was closer to my ultimate goal. If I lost, I went home.

The gymnasium was set up for a big tournament, with two boxing rings in the middle, surrounded by various tables and stations. There were tables for officials and a few for refs. There was also an area for judges to gather and a room for doctors and people helping at the weigh-in. Someone had to ring the bell, and there was an announcer. The crowd began to fill the bleachers. The concession stand workers started grilling sausages with peppers and onions. That's the usual setup for these kinds of events.

Since I was a little hungry, I was noticing the smell of all the food—everything, even kids opening chocolate bars.

Jesiah had decided the day before the fight that he wasn't going to come with us—he was sick of being dragged around to gyms.

"When is it going to be my turn to fight?" he had asked Papi the previous morning.

"When you're ready," Papi had said.

"I'm ready now!"

"No. You're not. But I'm sure your heart is ready. You need to get physically and mentally ready—that's just what you need to do to be ready. Your heart, you're born with that . . . but you need a little more time to grow."

"But only just a little more time . . ." Jesiah said.

Papi smiled. "Yes only just a little more time."

My father had scheduled a haircut appointment for himself at 9:00 p.m. that same night at J.C. Barbershop— the only time he could fit it into his schedule these days. He had left Jesiah at home with Grandma and taken me with him. I wasn't tired anyway and loved the alone time it offered us. Sometimes our best talks were in the car running errands together without my little brother around.

"Papi, when are you going to take Jesiah seriously about his boxing?"

"When he's willing to take it seriously. I see him at the gym, half training, half goofing off." Then he added thoughtfully, "With you, it was easy—you didn't want to do anything else but box. With Jesiah, he wants to try a lot of stuff, like football and baseball and karate . . . He's still figuring it out. But I don't want to force him into something he doesn't really want to do. He sees you boxing and thinks maybe that's what he needs to be doing, too . . . but he doesn't."

"And if he decides to box?"

"Then I'll help guide him the same way I helped guide you, Jess."

"Papi, I think some of the kids at school think I push too much to be a boxer."

He looked at me for a second. "Don't put any energy

into things that make you feel bad about things that you're doing that make you feel good about yourself."

"But do you think there's something wrong with it?"

"You're passionate and dedicated to a sport you love. I absolutely see nothing wrong with that."

At the tournament that day, it was just me, Papi, and Don. It was kind of nice to have my father to myself.

"Last call weigh-in," the female announcer said over the loudspeaker. "Last call weigh-in."

"I need lotion," I said to Papi. "You packed it, right?"

"Yes, and the Vaseline is in the side pocket. Put it on after weigh-in. Go."

I weighed in at 79 pounds, just under the 80-pound maximum for my division. I had pretty much starved myself that day to make sure I was just under. I had skipped breakfast *and* lunch and didn't drink anything before weigh-in.

My father knew I was hungry, so he left the gym and went searching for food.

Twenty minutes later, which seemed like an eternity, he came back and handed me a huge aluminum carryout container of my favorite dish—beans, rice, and avocado— from a restaurant nearby.

"Here you go . . . A nice hot plate of Spanish food and a decaf caramel Frappuccino from Starbucks."

I scarfed it down immediately. It was delicious! I loved it. And there was plenty of time before the fight to digest. My opponent, Molly, was a few pounds lighter but also made weigh-in, so the fight was officially on.

"Weigh-ins are closed," the announcer said over the loudspeaker.

There's a lot of waiting around before fights begin. This tournament's weigh-in started at 10:00 a.m., but the fights weren't set to start until 4:00 p.m.—even then they didn't start until 5:00 p.m. because of administrative stuff and getting boxers into the right categories and paired with the appropriate opponents. You'd be surprised how many no-shows, dropouts, and failed weigh-ins there are that complicate the process.

Papi always complained about the long wait between weigh-in and the fights. "I don't get it. What takes them so long? . . . These things are so disorganized . . . Why can't they figure out how to run these events more smoothly?" I could tell he was getting nervous. He would either talk too much or not at all when he was nervous.

As I was stretching, I overheard a boy next to me say to his teammate, "That's the kid I'm fighting over there."

His teammate said, "That scrawny kid?"

"Yeah, I'm beating him up today. I don't know who he is, but I'm beating him up."

(By the way, the kid who said that? He ended up losing. But that's a different story.)

A bunch of Irish boys had come down from Boston to fight. And a large group of teenaged boys from Syracuse. I didn't see many other girls fighting that day—maybe two others. Didn't matter: everyone in that room, every single one of us, was hungry for a win.

My gold, black, and purple uniform had been tucked in a storage bin long ago; now I wore the standard royal-blue jersey with an American flag and "USA" under it, and matching royal-blue boxing shorts that hung just below my knees. You're given pre-approved gloves—blue or red—and headgear. I trained with twelve-ounce gloves, but boxed in sanctioned matches with ten-ounce gloves. That way punching during a match came a little more easily.

headgear

10 oz gloves

standard jersey

As I was rubbing lotion on my body, my opponent was warming up.

"How does she look?" I asked Don, who was studying the competition.

"Her moves are sloppy. Her coach says she only trains two or three days a week."

Then I rubbed the Vaseline on my face, which helps the punches slip off.

"But don't worry about her," he said. "How are you feeling?"

"I feel good today. It helps to know who I'm fighting . . . Papi is at his best too when he knows my competition."

We looked over at my father, who was acting like his usual nervous self before a fight. Don and I laughed. "It will never get easier for him," Don said.

"Nope, never. He's the best," I said, smiling.

After a lot of waiting, we finally heard over the loudspeaker, "Welcome to the regional tournament for the Junior Olympics in Yonkers, New York. We have twenty-three exciting bouts for you this evening. As always, no yelling, screaming, swearing . . ." A bunch of kids laughed. "No fighting outside the ring. No flash photography. And now, please stand for our national anthem." One of the referees sang a very screechy version of "The Star-Spangled

Banner," but the sound kept cutting out because of the gym's old PA system, and once in a while the microphone feedback interrupted with a loud jarring hum and people covered their ears. Once the ref finished singing, the crowd went crazy cheering, but it made me wonder whether they were cheering because he was good or because they were glad the song was over.

Boxing events like PAL Nights are a totally different thing; even though they're sanctioned fights, and count as wins or loses on your record, they're not like regional tournaments . . . but you still need those smaller local matches to gain ring experience so you can perform on the bigger stage.

The announcer came on again. "Coaches, please have your book in hand. If you don't have your book, you can't work the corner . . ." A coach's book shows that they're registered under USA Boxing, and it's red. Fighters have books too—boxers' books are white. You need them to fight in a match. If you don't have your book, you can't fight. It's like a passport.

"Make sure your boxer has their shirt tucked in and a contrasting waistband. No pink, red, or orange mouth guards." Nothing that could make it hard to identify blood. A couple of fighters looked at their mouth guards. "And girls, make sure your hair is tucked into your headgear."

One boy jogged over to his mother. "I don't have another color mouth guard."

"Well, what are you gonna do?"

He started to freak out and ran over to his coach.

It was the same stuff every match—last-minute details and nerves that started to get the better of everybody, even the most seasoned fighters.

With that, the matches began in two separate rings. My fight was third—which I was thrilled about. It meant less waiting around and not enough time to have the butterflies build in my stomach, but just enough time to mentally focus on getting in the ring.

I was digging through my bag—soap to wash my hands, a bag of scrunchies, various creams, a change of clothing—when my father asked "How you doin', Jess?"

"I feel good. How are you doing?"

"Good. Good. Molly's a good kid. It'll be a solid fight. You're not nervous, are you?"

"Naaawww. Just a little nervous for Molly." I looked at my dad and laughed.

"You had some tough breaks from judges in the past," he said as I stretched my calves. "Some judges just aren't fair. That's why you can't leave it up to the judges to determine a fight. You have to go for a technical knockout if you want to win this thing. Okay?"

A boxer can receive a win by technical knockout—a TKO—in the amateurs by giving their opponent consistent eight-counts or just by knocking them out cold. TKOs are also given if an opponent gives up. People have asked me what it feels like to give a solid TKO, and I tell them that it's like all your emotions coming together—excited and happy but also a little worried for the other fighter. It's as exciting as it is scary.

Don was stretching me when over the loudspeaker I heard, "Jesselyn Silva to the glove table."

Don looked at me and I looked at him. "What do they want?" They called my name again: "Jesselyn Silva, please report to the glove table." I headed over, and a woman said, "We need your gloves back."

I was really confused. Don came to the table moments later and said, "What's up?"

"We need her gloves back."

"Why? She passed weigh-in."

"No, that's not it. There aren't enough gloves to go around. We need them for the first fight. She'll get them back afterward."

I panicked a little but Don reassured me that everything would be okay.

The judges took their places around the ring.

The announcer introduced the first two matches, and the fighting began. Papi helped secure my headgear. He tucked my baby hairs into the holes so no little strands were sticking out. He was so delicate about it. Then he gently kissed my forehead.

"Be smart, and *please* protect yourself at all times," he said to me.

"Protect yourself too," I said, smiling. It was a joke, because once Don had passionately kicked over a table after a bad decision and it had almost knocked out a parent on the bleachers near my father.

I did a lap around the gym to loosen up and then jabbed with Don. I laughed as he dodged my punches with ease. I felt relaxed and confident . . . but not too confident.

The bell rang, and the first two matches were over. One of the boys in the ring where I was about to fight was pointing to himself to declare his own victory, but the win went to the other boy. The guys from the Irish gym yelled foul play. "Judges called that one right," someone on the bleachers said.

A boy from the other ring walked over to me and threw his gloves at me. "Here. They said you needed these." (It was the boy who had said less than an hour ago so confidently that he was going to beat up his opponent.)

"Did you win?"

"Naw . . . lost. Cursed gloves. Good luck." He walked away.

"Matches three and four, get to your ring," the woman said over the loudspeaker.

"Okay, that's us," said Don. Papi gave me a gentle hug, and Don escorted me toward the ring. He rubbed my shoulders to relax me, and then gave me a few final words of encouragement. "You're going to be great out there. Just imagine what it will feel like to win and be one step closer to the Junior Olympics." It was my turn to enter the ring. My opponent entered from her corner. Our outfits were similar—blue shirts, blue shorts, matching approved head-gear. We were equals at the start.

We both stomped our feet at each side of the ring to acknowledge our respect for the judges.

The woman on the loudspeaker introduced our fight. "In ring number one, bout number three, the eighty-pound female division. Boxing out of the red corner, representing Metro, Molly Sullivan." [Cheers.] "And boxing in the blue corner, representing New Jersey, Jesselyn Silva." When she announced my name, I bounced up and down and pumped my fists in the air. I heard my father and a few other people in the crowd cheer.

"Eighty-pound female, three one-minute rounds, begin," finished the announcer.

We met in the middle and bumped fists. Then it was back to our corners. I heard a father say to his little girl in the bleachers, "They ain't playin' no games, right?"

The little girl said, "Go, girls!"

Don gave me a bunch of fist pumps. "You got this one, Jess!"

It seemed like forever before the bell rang. She came out fast, but I got the first few punches. Then she landed a hard right, but I got her back with a few solid uppercuts—enough to give her an eight-count. The bell rang, and I knew I had dominated the first round.

"You're doin' good, doin' good, keep it up," Don said. I drank some water and was up and bouncing, ready to get back in there. I looked over at Molly and could tell she was having a tough time. She was younger and less experienced, and I knew how

she was feeling. She slowly lifted herself up.

The bell rang and we were at it again. She was trying to dodge my punches, but I kept landing them. Another eight-count for my opponent. "Get your punches out faster," I could hear her coach saying.

> **I wanted this win. I wanted to make it to the championships.**

But her arms were getting tired, and I got inside her for a few more solid hits. The second round was over.

Papi gave me a big smile. "Nice work, Jess."

Round three and my mind was saying, *Go! Go!* I wanted this win. I wanted to make it to the championships. I'd never been to West Virginia. Why not now? The bell rang and I came out swinging and hit her hard. "There you go," Don said loudly.

Her coach was saying, "Get your balance. You got good balance. Stay with it." She landed a shot or two, and I heard her coach say, "That's my girl."

Then I got angry. *No,* I thought to myself. *There is going to be no doubt in the judges' minds this time. I'm going to win this completely.* So I went crazy with punches. I could hear Papi shouting, "Nice! Good job, Jess!" The ref called the fight because I had given the girl her third eight-count, which automatically gave me the win under the three-knock-down rule. It was done. The girl and I hugged and gave our signs of respect. Then I bumped fists with her coach.

When I took off my headgear, Don said, "That was some really good fighting. I'm very proud of you."

The decision had been delivered and the announcer came on. "In ring number one, bout number three, for the eighty-pound female Bantam division, your winner boxing out of the blue corner, Jesselyn Silva, representing New Jersey!" I raised my arms in victory.

I was heading to West Virginia.

CHAPTER TWELVE
ROAD TRIP AND THE
JUNIOR OLYMPICS

It's almost six hundred miles from Bergenfield, New Jersey, to Charleston, West Virginia. That meant I was going to be crammed in a car for over nine hours with Papi, Don, and my boxing teammate, Zack. I quickly came to realize that this road trip was going to be a different challenge of endurance: one of limbs falling asleep and foreign body odors and then of course the big issue of OPM . . . other people's music.

It was the end of June 2018, the summer before seventh grade. It had been a month since I fought Molly at the regional tournament in Yonkers, and since then, I had done nothing but prepare for the Junior Olympics, which meant focusing more at the gym, and less talking with my teammates. It also meant daily weigh-ins to make sure I wasn't gaining any weight.

The night before we left, I carefully packed my boxing outfits: my blue USA Boxing outfit, and my red ringside outfit with my white-and-blue HyperKO and neongreen HyperKO boxing shoes. Boxing shoes are one of the most important pieces of equipment a boxer owns, if not *the* most important piece. Good boxing shoes give you better control with your footwork and anchor your step. Bad ones make your feet slip, and you end up sore. I also packed my Everlast gloves for when we did mitt work for tune-ups. In mitt work, the coach holds mitts so that a boxer can work on combinations. It emulates a boxer throwing punches and helps a fighter work on slipping them. Finally, I packed my army socks. I always wore my army socks, because I was going to war. "Kill or be killed!"

That night I had a tough time sleeping because I kept thinking that I had forgotten to pack something. But I couldn't think of what, so every so often I'd jump out of bed, check my packing list, and double-check my bag. Then I'd throw one more thing in until my bag was busting at the seams.

We got on the road at 4:45 in the morning; I was super tired, and my mouth had that toothpaste taste in it that made me feel a little nauseated. It was the last day of classes before summer vacation, but I skipped school that day to head to nationals. All my teachers agreed it was a pretty good excuse to call in absent. My classmates and friends were very supportive as well. A few friends even wrote me notes of encouragement; I was a little sad not to be there on the final day before summer, but at the same time I was ready for the Junior Olympics, mentally and physically. All I could think about was the moment I would step into that ring and meet my opponent face-to-face.

The sun rising over sleeping cities looked like a huge bowl of sherbet. Jesiah loves sherbet, but his favorite ice cream flavor is Neapolitan—the kind with three flavors in one: chocolate, vanilla, and strawberry. He'd make sure to get a stripe of every flavor on his spoon before gobbling each bite.

I was going to miss him. The last words he said to me were "I hope you win!" Then he hugged me really tightly and said, "Good luck . . . Now good night!"

It was one of those warm, sunny mornings when you'd rather be at the beach than in the car for a whole day—but "Better this than snow," Papi said. Even without the snow, traffic was slow, sometimes at a standstill for what seemed like forever. And you know how it is when you want to get someplace: standing still seems like an eternity.

208 MY CORNER OF THE RING

"If it's not bad weather, it's road construction," Zack mumbled next to me.

"Come on, guys! We're on the open road!" Don said with a fist pump. The car burst into laughter. That was at hour one . . . By hour four, we seemed to be in just stop-and-go traffic.

I'd been playing a game with Zack, but he'd gotten tired of it. Zack was sixteen years old, tall, and really strong. He'd just moved to Englewood, New Jersey, from Philadelphia, so he was still getting to know people. Boxing helped him meet some kids. He'd been boxing for two years. He dozed off pretty quickly, and Don tried to get a funny photo of him sleeping to tease him later.

Papi and I thought we were going to get some rest on the drive, but Coach Don saw my father nodding off and shouted jokingly, "Pedro, this is no time to sleep. We're going to the nationals!" Then he began to sing at the top of his lungs whenever he saw anybody closing their eyes for too long. I think he just didn't want to be the only one awake while driving.

"Come on, Jess, gotta keep your eyes open to see the world," he said.

It was true: the only way to really see the world is to keep your eyes wide open and study what's in front of you. I saw mountains so tall that I had to crane my neck out the window to see the tops of them. And fields of grass that went as far as the eye could see. But what was most interesting to me were all the trucks on the road. Papi and I would try to guess what all those trucks were carrying.

Don told us that one of the best parts about being a boxer is the amount of travel you do for each tournament. He'd traveled all over the place when he was an amateur boxer—to places like Las Vegas and Florida and even other countries.

"I wouldn't have seen any of those places had I not been heading to another tournament," he said.

He looked in his rearview mirror at Zack, who had been playing *Fortnite* on his phone most of the drive. "Might not seem like much when you're in the moment," Don said, addressing the entire car, "but appreciate these long drives. They happen in the blink of an eye." It wasn't just new places; it was also new people, new experiences, breaking up the routine of life that was the best part of the adventure.

I must admit, all the distractions of being surrounded by my father, my coach, and my teammate were a nice break from thinking about the

> **The only way to really see the world is to keep your eyes wide open and study what's in front of you.**

tournament ahead. I tried not to think of all the things that could go wrong, like losing, and imagined what it would feel and look like to win. Don always told us to "imagine the win." Of course he gave us tips the entire road trip and told us about his first fights and going to nationals.

"You know, Jess and Zack," said Don, "you two are the first Junior Olympians in our gym to go to the nationals. This is a very big deal. You know that, right?"

Zack just kind of nodded and went back to playing *Fortnite*, and I started to laugh.

"Yeah, Don, we know it's a big deal . . . We're just in the zone. Not getting too excited, you know?"

He knew. He trained us to stay relaxed and focused. Like Jedis, Jesiah would say.

Then somewhere in D.C., we got lost. Don's bits of wisdom and silly stories quickly changed to confusion, then silence. We all looked around with wide eyes. But looking back, I think Don might have gotten lost on purpose. Because after we drove in what seemed to be endless circles around the District, we somehow, miraculously, pulled up to the White House. The White House! And stopped. "Wow," "Oh man," "So cool," we all said at once. Don grinned a wide grin. It was beyond amazing to be right in front of something I'd only seen in photographs. Now I was in photographs with it.

As we got back on the road, the GPS took us half an hour in the wrong direction. But it was well worth the detour. While Don tried to get us unlost, we all rode in silence. Then he returned to singing, and we all told stories. Around that time, I started to miss home . . . Mostly I missed my brother and wished he were going to the nationals with us.

I also kept thinking about the look on my grandma's face when I left. She had clutched my hands together and said a little prayer, and when she hugged me, she told me to keep my head up . . . something she'd heard my father say over and over again about boxing. I knew she was still uncomfortable with having a granddaughter who boxed, but I also knew she was proud of me. "Not many grandmothers can say they have a granddaughter going to fight in the Junior Olympics," I'd overheard her say to one of her friends on the phone. It was a good reminder of how far I had come in this sport. Sometimes when you're so involved in something, you forget where you started from. This was a long way from The Jim in Edgewater, New Jersey, five years ago. Getting to where I was now had taken years of dedication and hard work in the gym.

"Wake up, everyone," Don said a few hours later. "No more sleeping!"

"Sleep is underrated," Zack said, stretching and yawning.

"We're here."

"We're here?"

We arrived in Charleston, West Virginia, that same day late in the afternoon. It was quieter than I expected. Given that it was a city of 50,000 people, I thought there would be bustle. But very few people were on the streets the day we arrived. "I think it's the heat," said Don. It was dreadfully hot. We found a gas station and asked how far the Civic Center was. Turns out it was nearby. The Civic Center was where the nationals were being held, and Don wanted Zack and me to see it before the tournament began. I'm glad we did, because the place was enormous and I wanted to explore it. It's a 13,500-seat coliseum with a two-story lobby and a huge center arena . . . and I was going to be boxing there!

"Don't let the grandness intimidate you," Don said to me with a smile. "That boxing ring is the same size as the one back home. Same exact dimensions, same exact height off the ground."

After we checked in to the tournament, I got all my information. The most exciting thing I learned was who my roommate was going to be for the weekend! At regionals, the makeup of your team is based on your gym, but when you go to a national tournament, it's based on the state you live in and represent. Because I was on Team Jersey, I got to meet some pretty cool boxers from my state. My room-mate was a girl named Elizabeth. She'd been to nationals five times, so I asked her a zillion questions about what to expect. She was sixteen years old and super focused on her fights when she was at tournaments, but outside tourna-ments she was crazy-funny and caring.

Her cousins were there boxing as well, and they were rooming next to us: Los, Jeremiah, Chinny, and Narem. It felt a little weird being with so many kids my age who loved to talk about boxing, but it certainly kept my mind from worrying about nationals. We hung out playing *Grand Theft Auto* and watching cartoons until the adults came in.

"Everyone get to bed early tonight. You have a big day tomorrow," Elizabeth's coach (who's also her father) told us.

But when the doors closed, Elizabeth said, "Do you like water sports?"

"Yeah," I said, a little confused. Her cousins started to laugh.

"Good! Because we have a game we like to play. Whoever falls asleep first tonight is going to get cold water poured on their face. And if you fall asleep first again, then you get toothpaste."

Guess who fell asleep first . . . And then again. So I was the one who got both the water and the toothpaste treatment. I didn't get much sleep that night, but I did have a lot of fun.

Papi and I got to the weigh-ins super early—6:00 a.m.— with Elizabeth and her father. I weighed in at 79.4, just within the 80-pound division. Then I waited and watched for my opponent to arrive . . . and I waited. The line of boxers for that day got smaller and smaller. My opponent never showed. Don was furious. "We didn't come all this way to win by forfeit!" And with that, he stormed off to talk to the people running the tournament. He came back a few minutes later with a serious look on his face.

"Well, I talked to the officials, and they said because your opponent never showed, she gets disqualified and you automatically win the division with a gold medal." Don, my father, and I all looked at one another with concern. That's not how I wanted to win a medal—because a girl never showed, so I never fought but won anyway?

"I came here to fight, Don," I said.

"Well, the other option is that you could fight up in the 85-pound division," Don replied.

"Yes!" I responded.

"But I should warn you, Jess, some of those girls are pretty tough and have a lot more experience."

"I don't see that as a problem, I see that as a challenge," I said.

"I feel the same way." Don was smiling.

Papi said nothing but looked a little nervous, as usual. And we all laughed.

I had to wait a full day to weigh in for the 85-pound division. But the fun part was that I got to eat a really big breakfast and an even bigger lunch to compete at the higher weigh-in. I also got to watch a lot of incredible boxing.

The level of boxing at nationals is the best in the nation— only the top winners of each division make it there—so competition was the highest I'd ever seen. Everyone was out to win. And what I learned was that if it was your first time at nationals—like it was mine—you have to full-blown beat your opponent for the judges to notice you and give you the decision. Otherwise you'll probably get robbed. At least that was my opinion and the opinion of my teammates.

"Jess, you gotta do the best fighting of your life here," Don told me. "The judges need to recognize you as an experienced boxer so there's no second-guessing who won or lost the fight."

I understood what I needed to do—bring full heat!

The next morning was another early one, and I was more ready than ever and up for the challenge. But this time at the trial scale (the scale that checks your weight before you get onto the actual scale to determine if you might come in over weight) the place wasn't quiet, calm, and empty like it had been the first day—it was packed and the level of anxiety loomed large in the room.

I waited for about twenty minutes in line at weigh-in. The girls in line were nervous and excited. We all asked each other questions like where we were from, how we all got here, where we trained, and how much time we dedicated to boxing. There were lots of funny stories. One girl said that when she gets nervous, she gets too much saliva in her mouth and needs to spit a lot—so she kept spitting into a cup, which made everyone a little uncomfortable.

I weighed in at 81.2 pounds, which qualified me for the division.

The brackets went up later that day in the Civic Center hallway—it was a list of about 75 female boxers from all over the country. I found out I was boxing a girl named Lauren from Tennessee. I had heard about her because she'd been to the nationals ten times and was a ten-time nationals champion. Her current boxing record was 23-0 . . . meaning she hadn't lost a single fight. She was this beautiful African American girl with long, curly brown hair and bright eyes. She was heavier and taller than I was, which made her even more intimidating.

Don wasn't too thrilled to have to start the nationals

with such an experienced boxer, but I reminded him that I had come there to fight. "We didn't travel all this way to fight easy fights; we came here to battle for the title." That was how I saw it.

The moment Lauren and I got into the ring, we stared each other down. I was boxing out of the blue corner, and she was boxing out of the red corner. Her eyes were saying, *I'm gonna kill you*, but so were mine. And in the ring her height or weight didn't scare me. I felt more determined and just as prepared. My body felt strong that day, and my punches felt smooth. To me, this was just as even a match as any.

We stomped our feet at the judges to show our respect to them, and for the first time in my experience of fighting in matches, I noticed that when my opponent stomped to the judges, they all smiled at her because they knew who she was. When I stomped, there were no smiles and there was no recognition of who I was. I knew right then and there that it would be an uphill battle to prove myself.

When I came back to my corner, I said to Don, "Did you see the judges smiling at her?"

"Don't worry, Jess," he said. "By the time you're done fighting her, they'll remember who you are. No doubt in my mind they'll remember you."

The ref checked my blue mouth guard, my blue head-gear, my blue gloves. He was friendly and gave my shoulders a kind squeeze for good luck. I bounced up and down and shook my arms and legs to stay relaxed.

The announcer came on the loudspeaker—it was a huge venue, and the announcer's voice echoed throughout the whole arena. It was pretty cool! He announced Lauren in the red corner first, and I heard a burst of applause. She had a much bigger fan base, for sure. Then my name in the blue corner was announced, and the only people I heard clapping were my father, Don, Elizabeth's dad, and a couple of teammates. The difference in the level of applause actually made me chuckle a little. *Guess I should have brought my own cheering section*, I thought.

We bumped fists and I said good luck. I heard a bunch of people shouting, "Let's go, Lauren!" and "All right, Lauren, this one's yours!" Don gave me the usual quick words of encouragement, and then it was go time. I didn't take my eyes off Lauren until the bell rang. She kept her eyes down instead of looking at me, which was unusual for a boxer. We both shot out

quickly, but I got the first punch, a quick jab. It felt good to start out that way. In the first round we were feeling each other out, testing each other a little, throwing softballs. I was figuring out her stance and noticed she wasn't south-paw like me, since she was a little bigger and had a strut where she kept her head down with her eyes focused on the floor. Most boxers are trained to keep their heads up, their eyes on their opponent. She was seeing me, I could tell, but not with the usual stare-down I was familiar with in other boxers. Almost immediately I knew she was strong, but not stronger than me. *I got this*, I told myself. And before I knew it, the bell to the first round rang and I went back to my corner. Don brought the stool over the ropes for me to sit on and said, "Listen: you're moving well, and your punches look good. Don't think about her size or her experience. You got yourself here because you're a solid fighter. Focus on your moves. Okay?"

This was a bigger venue, and I was more nervous than usual. "Okay . . . okay," I said, taking in Don's words. *I got myself here because I can fight.*

"Good. Keep it up," he said, and he gave me a gentle whack with the towel.

I was eager to get back out there and show this girl, and the world, what I could do.

POW!
POW!
POW! POW!
POW!

The second bell rang. Lauren came hard and got in the first punch and then a few more, but I slipped and ducked most of them, got my balance, then came back with a few punches of my own. I was getting in my groove and got inside her enough to dodge most of her hits. I noticed she overexaggerated her left-hand punch, so I played on that weakness by making her work her left side more. I got her on the ropes and made her miss about five punches. I waited for her to come at me, slowed the pace, moved her off her timing, and then made her pay with a few hard punches.

After the second bell rang, ending the round, I walked over to my corner and slowly exhaled. I felt like I had a chance to win. I wanted to win. I had come to win. I said that to Don. "Then go for it," he said. "Make this third round the best of your life." He whacked my headgear and said, "Win or lose, I'm so proud of you. You look fantastic up there. Okay? You look really strong."

"Yeah, yeah." I nodded. Strength. Dedication. Hard work. Passion.

He drizzled cold water down my back from a water bottle, and I could feel it trail like little snakes down my spine. Don told me to focus on my breathing. "Keep pressuring her. Move and make her miss. She's not used to that style of boxing."

As I listened to him, I heard one of my teammates yell, "Come on, Jess, you're so close!" He was right. I was so close. Close up and examining the world of boxing at the national level from the inside now. In this huge arena, with all these people watching and fans cheering; lights, camera, action. No more dreaming of this day: this day was here! This is what it meant to be a champion fighter.

In the blink of an eye, the third bell rang for the third and final round, and I went for it. I said to myself, *Go for it. NOW!* I came out not straight at her, but more slowly and to her left side. Five quick jabs, then a straight left. I was up before the round really started, and it caught her off guard. Then she went all nuts too, and we were both going crazy with the punches. In my mind I said, *One-two, one-two.* I just kept going after her. I threw everything into the ring that day—my entire body, my mind let loose. Everything opened, and I felt free, strong, determined to be my best. The bell rang, and the

" I felt free, strong, determined to do my best. "

two of us hugged in exhaustion. It was over. I'd done my best, and now it was up to the judges to decide.

In fights like these, you never know which way the decision will go. I thought I was going to win, but I said to myself that whether I won or lost, it didn't matter: I had done my best work and could carry my head high. We stood together with the ref between us. Before the decision was called, I pointed to the blue corner, signaling that I thought the win should go to me. This is a common practice used by fighters to say to the judges that they think they deserve the win. I deserved the win! A few minutes seemed like forever. Then finally, they announced it over the speaker. "Ladies and gentlemen, your winner, boxing out of the red corner . . ."

It took me a second to process. The red corner . . . not the blue corner.

I had lost.

I won't say I felt like I was robbed, but I did think I had done just as good a job boxing that day. And it wasn't all bad. I ended the nationals with a bronze. Lauren ended up winning the gold. Not bad for my first time.

After the fight, Lauren's mom came up to me and said I was the toughest opponent her daughter had ever had and that after the first round, she was nervous even watching, which had never happened to her before.

On the drive home, we talked about our experiences and the fights of other teammates. Zack had lost, and Elizabeth had lost, too. The others I had met that weekend didn't do much better than bronzes. I told my father, Don, and Zack that getting a bronze was okay, but that next year I was going back for gold.

CHAPTER THIRTEEN
BEING A GIRL MY OWN WAY

When I got home from the nationals, the first person to greet me at the door was Jesiah. He cheered, "You're number one! You're number one!" As I walked in the door, I said, "I didn't win in my division, Jesiah."

"You're still number one," he said without skipping a beat.

"Jesselyn, we are all so proud of you." My grandmother's voice was warm and gentle.

"I brought home the bronze." I proudly held up my medal.

"I heard you fought hard and well against one of the strongest competitors in the division. You represented your family well."

"And Don's gym . . . and your state . . . and girls everywhere," said Papi, carrying in two heavy bags from our trip.

"I wanted to come home with the gold."

"But you know, Jesiah is right: you are number one in
many ways," my grandmother said. "You are the first in
our family to make it to the Junior Olympics, and you are
the first to already have accomplished so much in your
lifetime." She smiled. "And you're still so young! So many
firsts lie ahead, so be patient."

My grandmother was right. Maybe I hadn't come home
with the gold, but I had done something that felt important
and big for me and my family. It made me feel very special
inside, and all that hard work felt worth it.

It was nice to be back in my own bedroom—although I
had loved having a roommate for a few days. I walked over
to my dream calendar. I had not accomplished my last goal
of winning the Junior Olympics . . . but instead of crossing
it out, I put a check next to it. "Accomplished!" I had won
even if I hadn't won.

I looked at all the things I had completed on my dream
calendar and decided it was time to start a new set of goals.
I grabbed a piece of paper and started to jot down ideas.
But what was going to be on my list this time? Win more
fights, work out every day, run three miles . . . I had to

think. I knew. I wrote. "Wake up every day a stronger person." Then I wrote under that: "OLYMPICS 2024 . . . Bring home the gold!"

★ ★ ★

I GOT A call from Everlast a week after the Junior Olympics. A nice woman named Sidney from the company said she had heard about my fight in West Virginia and had checked out my Instagram account.

"We at Everlast are very impressed with your accomplishments!" Her voice was peppy. "You're a real inspiration for a lot of young ladies."

We had a long talk about boxing and being a girl in a male-dominated sport and about commitment and never giving up. "What drives you to be your best?" she asked.

"I don't know. I drive myself," I said without even considering any other answer. "A lot of people don't like to see girls in combat sports. It makes them uncomfortable. But for me it's the place that makes me feel most comfortable."

"Why, do you think?" she said with genuine curiosity.

"Well, a lot of things are done on the surface. Fighting forces me to go deeper. I like to challenge my physical and emotional limits, and boxing does that for me in ways that nothing else does."

"Jesselyn, you are exactly the kind of person Everlast is making sports equipment for. Thank you for sharing your thoughts with me."

A few days after our first phone conversation, I got a package from her with brand-new Everlast wraps—red ones, blue ones, and some with gold polka dots—as well as boxing gloves and an Everlast backpack, which I liked the best of all.

A note inside said, "Jess, you are all about what Everlast wants to encourage in its athletes. Keep working hard. I hope these help you win gold in the Junior Olympics next year!"

A few days after the package arrived, I got another phone call from Sidney. She asked if I had liked the care package. I said, "Of course! I've never had so much cool gear. Thank you! But you know, I didn't win in my division at Junior Olympics . . ."

She chuckled a little and said, "You are inspiring, Jess, win or lose, and we'd like you to share your story with our help."

Before I knew it, I was heading down Spruce Street in Paterson, New Jersey, a few weeks later looking for the Art Factory. I had agreed to make a video and do an ad for Everlast, and they had emailed the address and told me to be there by 9:00 a.m. We pulled up to the location and it was this old warehouse—a four-story brick building with red doors and some graffiti on a few walls. It was so interesting from the outside that I couldn't wait to see what it looked like on the inside.

The first thing I noticed inside were the elevators. They were the old-style ones with no door or gate; they were more like big freight elevators, where you push a lever down to go up. Jesiah laughed and laughed at the thought of cranking something down to go up.

Sidney met us at the elevator. She was just as warm and friendly in person. "Welcome to Everlast's 'Be First' campaign!" The space was a large open room with dirty wooden floors. Cameras and lights were set up everywhere, and as we entered, they were in the middle of a photo shoot with a dancer named Liz Marie who was involved in the same Be First campaign. She was wearing a really cool dance outfit, and they kept making her do these graceful leaps. "Again," said the videographer. So she'd leap again and again effortlessly.

As we made our way past the dancer, another woman came over to me and said, "Welcome, Jesselyn! I'll be doing your hair and makeup."

"Makeup?!" I pulled back.

"Ha ha! Nothing too over the top, I promise. Maybe just some face moisturizer and lip balm."

"Yeah, nothing that, you know, makes her look too grown-up," my father said firmly.

The makeup artist laughed and said, "Of course not. It will be age appropriate, I promise."

"And we have this for you as well," Sidney said, handing me an Everlast T-shirt with "Jesszilla" on the sleeve.

"Am I wearing this in the video?" I asked with excitement.

With that, another crew member came over and said, "You'll be wearing a number of outfits for the video and camera shoot. I'll be doing your wardrobe. Come on, let's have some fun!"

The experience was straight out of a dream. I had one person dressing me, one person putting lotion on my face, and another person going over my lines with me.

For the video, my hair was done in a cool ponytail split to the side. My hair had never smelled so good! First they dressed me in a blue shirt and black tights. I did a number of poses and action shots. Then I switched outfits, this time to a peach shirt and hot-pink Everlast shoes. More action photos. I jumped rope and walked around the warehouse while they took pictures and videotaped me. Up the

stairs, down the stairs. Serious face, boxing face, smiling face, funny face. I jumped rope, I hit the bag, I sprinted, I shadowboxed. I found out two of my favorite pro fighters were also part of the Be First campaign: Deontay Wilder and Mikaela Mayer.

Then I was given a piece of paper and told to memorize what was on it. The words were like poetry, and I loved saying them over and over again.

"Now, look into the camera, and say your lines." I wasn't

used to staring directly at the camera, but I did. It felt like I was staring into the soul of something big and vast. With seriousness I said:

Never been done by someone like me.

I had to be first.

It was my only option.

But it wasn't just for me, you see.

I broke the ground.

My will, my strength obliterated

What was set in stone.

And now I sit on this throne.

Slip move and counter.

Who got next?! It don't matter.

Dictate the pace.

All fears are erased.

Let 'em see how it's done.

Let 'em watch the real one.

Had to teach them my worth.

Had to choose to be first.

The lines of my script described it perfectly. Being first wasn't about coming in first place. It was about being the first person to do it in your own unique way. I was creating my own rules. I had shown up. I was a boxer training out of Hackensack, New Jersey. I taught people how to do a few things and sometimes I won, sometimes I lost. I broke the ground with mighty force, and now I could dictate my own pace. I was a girl my way, in my corner of the ring.

GLOSSARY

AMATEUR BOXING: Competitive boxing where neither participant is paid and most fighters are beginning to learn their craft.

BE FIRST: When your coach tells you to "be first," they want you to throw your punches before your opponent. In other terms, he or she wants you to be aggressive.

BLOCK: A defensive move of the hands, arms, and shoulders to stop punches from landing on the face or body.

BLOW, OR PUNCH: A strike or hit with a clenched fist.

BOB AND WEAVE: Side to side and rolling movements that are used as defense to avoid punches. Heavyweight Mike Tyson is a classic example of someone who used the bob and weave defense to perfection.

BOUT, OR MATCH: A boxing contest taking place as part of a competition.

BOXING GLOVES: Protective padded coverings for the hands, usually made of leather.

BOXING INSIDE / OUTSIDE: The terms inside and outside are used in boxing to describe punching distance. For instance, outside fighting is when the fighter remains on the outside edge of an opponent's punching range. Inside fighting is staying within your opponent's range of attack. This is the most dangerous range, because it's where both boxers are able to deal damage to each other. It's also known as fighting "in the pocket," and if both boxers are fighting in the pocket long enough, it's known as fighting "toe-to-toe."

BOXING RING: A space in which a boxing match is held. A modern ring, which is set on a raised platform, is square with a post at each corner. Four parallel rows of ropes are attached to the posts using turnbuckles, devices used for adjusting the tension or length of the ropes.

BREAK: This is a command used by a boxing referee to stop the action and separate the fighters.

COMBINATION: A series of punches thrown in sequence without a break.

COUNTERPUNCH: A punch thrown in response to an opponent's punch.

COVER UP: This is a defensive move employed by a fighter to avoid getting hit. He or she simply hides beneath and behind their gloves to avoid direct contact from an offensive attack.

CROSS: A straight power punch thrown with the rear hand, which travels across the fighter's body.

DEFENSE: Aspect of boxing which aims for complete evasion of an opponent's punches.

EIGHT-COUNT: When one fighter is knocked down or in danger of being stopped by a series of punches, a referee can administer a count of eight to give the fighter time to recover or so that he or she can better assess the situation.

EXHIBITION BOUT: A competitive match in which a winner is declared but the result is not officially recorded.

FEINT: A fake movement or punch used to make an opponent unnecessarily react, or to draw attention from one's actual point of attack.

GO TO THE BODY: An offensive strategy focused on attacking the midsection or abdominal region, as opposed to targeting the head.

HAND WRAPS: Strips of cloth used by boxers to protect hands and wrists against injuries induced by punching.

HEADGEAR: A padded helmet worn on the head by contestants in amateur and Olympic boxing for protection.

HOOK: This punch is thrown with the lead or front hand and is delivered in a semicircular pattern. The hook is executed by leading with the front hand, bringing the elbow up, and rotating the front side of the body (in a similar motion as slamming a door). It is meant to reach beyond an opponent's guard and make contact with the side of his or her head or chin.

JAB: A punch that is thrown with the front hand and delivered straight at the opponent. It should be the centerpiece of any boxing offense.

JUDGE: An individual whose job is to be present at ringside to score a bout and assign points to the boxers, based on punches that connect and overall performance.

OFFENSE: A technique that relies heavily on punching.

ORTHODOX: A fighting stance where the boxer has their left hand and left foot forward, leading with left jabs, and following with a right cross left hook. It is the normal stance for a right-handed boxer.

REFEREE: The individual charged with enforcing the rules during a match.

RINGSIDE: A spectator position in the front row or right next to the ring.

ROUNDS: Time periods in a boxing match for fighting, separated by one-minute breaks.

SANCTION: A certificate of approval issued by USA Boxing for events/matches.

SLIP: To move one's head to avoid getting hit.

SOUTHPAW: A fighting stance where the boxer has their right hand and right foot forward, leading with right jabs, and following with a left cross right hook. It is the normal stance for a left-handed boxer.

SPAR: To engage in a training match used to gain experience in preparation for a sanctioned bout.

SPONSOR: A person or organization that provides funds or goods for a project or activity carried out by another.

STICK AND MOVE: This is an offensive style of fighting that incorporates a great deal of movement, with the fighter constantly punching and moving.

TECHNICAL KNOCKOUT (TKO): The termination of a fight when a fighter has been declared by the referee unable to safely continue after having received too many blows, or due to appearing too unsteady after three eight-counts.

TOE-TO-TOE: When two fighters stand directly in front of each other and exchange punches at close range without backing away.

UPPERCUT: A punch thrown in an upward fashion, through the middle of a fighter's guard, intended to make impact on the point of his chin. It is delivered from a crouched position, with the hands up and, as the upper torso twists, the hand is extended out and up slightly to make contact. This can be thrown with either hand.

USA BOXING: The national governing body for all Olympic-style amateur boxing in the United States. It is overseen by the United States Olympic Committee and the International Boxing Association (AIBA).

WEIGH-IN: Pre-fight meeting for boxers to be weighed to make sure they are within their weight class limits.

WEIGHT CLASSES: Competition divisions based on weight limits. For example *bantamweight*, which has an upper limit of 118 pounds for professionals and 119 pounds for amateurs.

ACKNOWLEDGMENTS

I am so grateful for all the amazing people who worked on this book with me. Thank you for being in my corner! Dear God, I would like to thank you for giving me life daily and the strength and abilities to overcome any obstacles set before me. To my dad, mother, and the rest of my family, I want to thank you guys for always believing in me and supporting me every step of the way. To Coach Don and the rest of my boxing family, thank you for accepting me on my first day in the gym and motivating me every day. Forever dedicated!

Who would have thought I could be an author of my own book at twelve years old? I would like to thank Saira Rao and Carey Albertine at In This Together Media; Jess Regel at Foundry Literary + Media; Brin Stevens, my co-writer; and Stacey Barney at Penguin Random House for your help making this dream a reality. I couldn't have asked for a better team for this project. Thank you!

Thank you to all my supporters on social media who are always showing me love. And thanks to all the doubters for giving me the extra push to do my best!

I need to get through the last set of push-ups at the end of my workout. I will remain forever grateful for everything and everyone that has been part my journey. See you guys at the 2024 Olympics! To be continued . . .

PHOTO AND ART CREDITS